ESSAYS ON EDUCATION

ESSAYS ON EDUCATION

BY ALFRED WHITNEY GRISWOLD

PRESIDENT OF YALE UNIVERSITY

NEW HAVEN: YALE UNIVERSITY PRESS, 1954

London: Geoffrey Cumberlege, Oxford University Press

Printed in the United States of America by
Vail-Ballou Press, Inc., Binghamton, N. Y.

Several of these essays have appeared in the Atlantic
Monthly, the Georgia Review, Harper's Magazine,
the New York Herald Tribune, the New York Times, and
the Saturday Review. Thanks are due to them for
permission to reprint here.
First published, February, 1954; second printing, May, 1954
Library of Congress catalog card number: 54-5548.

TO MY COLLEAGUES

IN THE TEACHING PROFESSION

AT YALE AND ELSEWHERE.

Preface

The essays that comprise this book were written in the course of duty during my first three years in an office that affords all too little opportunity for literary effort. Most of them were delivered as addresses on various formal academic occasions. They are printed here without revision save for the omission of some local detail. Such unity as they may possess is the unity of variations on a theme. Their conclusions are for the reader to judge after he has read them, not for the writer to suggest in the hope of a favorable judgment.

I hope, though, that the reader will allow me a word or two concerning the mood in which these pages were written. For he will detect a sense, and here and there a note, of irony that so much of their space should be taken up with a justification of our colleges and universities, with the right of these institutions to carry on the work enjoined upon them by their charters and the provision of material means to make that possible. When I was a student at Yale and afterward during my first years as a member of the faculty, such matters were taken for granted. The towers and campuses of colleges and universities appeared fixed landmarks in the American scene, their lore pervasive in American thought and custom. Although our own futures in the depression-ridden 'thirties might (and did) concern us, the future of Yale seemed so secure as to be uninteresting. In fact, in these years, the experience of college and the recollection of that experience formed one of the few elements of stability in the life of many a disoriented and frustrated individual. That such foundations as these could be shaken seemed out of the question.

Yet shaken they were, and we can still feel the tremors. War with its passions, its aftermath of fear and hate, its crushing debt, has shaken our whole society to its foundations, and our colleges and universities have not escaped this cosmic disturbance. How long will it continue? What effects will it have upon our national system of education and the national character that is molded by that system? The reader of this volume will discover that I have no final answers to these questions. But he will be encouraged to face the questions and will, I hope, gain some realization of the degree to which they have distracted higher education and still threaten to divert it from its proper course.

During the past three years American education has become ever more deeply involved in a crisis the proportions and probable consequences, indeed the very existence, of which are largely unsuspected. The crisis is compounded of three immediate factors: a rapidly increasing population, failure to provide educational facilities in proportion, and the decline of the liberal arts. The first two factors express themselves in overcrowded schools, teacher shortages, the breakdown of discipline, and general deterioration of the quality of instruction. Our indifference to the liberal arts has resulted in widespread confusion and corruption of curricular standards.

In his discourse *Learning Makes Men Happier Than Ignorance,* Milton declares that "the man who knows nothing of the liberal arts seems to be cut off from all access to the happy life." I believe this proposition to be as true and valid today as it was when Milton stated it or the Greeks first thought it. It is borne out in the unpoetic language of modern psychiatry which finds a significantly higher incidence of nervous disorders among uneducated than among educated persons. The liberal arts are no panacea. They are not for every student in the same form and in equal measure. But just as an individual is poorer without them, so is a system of education. A system of education in which they become confused with substitutes and lost in the shuffle is not in good health. Such is the case with ours.

From one or more of these evils—the overcrowding, the shortage of teachers, the deterioration of quality and corruption of standards—hardly a school, college, or university in this country has escaped. Nor for that matter have many American homes.

If we were as attentive to educational trends as we have learned to be to our business cycle, we would have been prompt to recognize these evils and strike at their roots. We would have foreseen the needs of education and produced the resources and skills to meet them. At all events we would not have allowed those needs to gain such a lead on us as they have. The efforts we are and have been making to provide the buildings and equipment, the properly trained and qualified teachers, the curricular improvements commensurate with our educational ideals, would have been many times magnified and, by now, many times more effective.

What have we been doing instead? We have been

looking for skeletons in the closet. We have found a few —proper skeletons, for the most part, relics of an era that is past—abject or defiant though they may have been when brought to light. On the whole I think they prove the weakness and failure of their erstwhile cause rather than its strength and success. That these deluded critics, most of them now repentant, made no more of an impression on our teaching profession and our educational system than has been established to date is one more proof of the essential soundness of our way of life and the honesty and common sense of the American people, whatever their profession.

Scouting the skeletons from their closets has not met the crisis in American education. It has been a diversion, to some extent, maybe, an excuse for avoiding it. It has even worsened the crisis by spilling over in indiscriminate vengeance upon the whole teaching profession and so discouraging self-respecting citizens from entering it. It has done nothing to remedy the basic evils besetting American education which, if allowed to continue much longer might easily refill the closets, this time with enemies of our society with flesh on their bones.

The reader may wonder why higher education should be affected by troubles that seem for the moment to be concentrated in primary and secondary schools. In a few years, when the school children of today reach college age, he will no longer have cause to wonder. So far as school, college, and university are concerned educational standards are indivisible. If one of these institutions fails, all fail. The institutions of higher education cannot maintain their standards if the schools do not send them properly qualified students. If those students are crowded and hustled through undisciplined classrooms, taught by overworked, underpaid, and inadequately trained teachers, and nurtured on subjects that do not constantly stretch their minds and enlarge their vision, it is illusory to believe that either the liberal arts colleges or the graduate and professional schools of universities can maintain their standards.

This is not to say that the colleges and universities have no troubles of their own, much less that they are exempt from responsibility for the troubles of the schools. Because I happen to live and work in a university the reader will find a good bit about the troubles of universities in the pages that follow. As for the universities' responsibility to the schools, it is direct and vital. For their own sakes I believe that all of them, Yale in particular, should be helping the schools in every possible way, especially with the recruitment and training of teachers and the organization and content of curricula.

But to do that the universities must be provided the kind and quantity of resources they need: the lame cannot shoulder the halt. The whole complex must first be perceived by society and understood for what it is—the mind and spirit of American democracy in danger of its life. And how can it see this in an exhibit of skeletons?

This obsession with skeletons is morbid. It has to do with hate and fear and death. American education has to do with hope and courage and life. The feeling of being constantly distracted by the morbid from the vital has been very much with me as I wrote these pages, and accounts for their note of irony. Yet if they should incline the reader's thoughts and actions to the living needs of American education and the infinite promise fulfillment of those needs holds for our country and for the world, that feeling will be dispelled and my labors well repaid.

A. W. G.

Martha's Vineyard
September, 1953

Contents

Inaugural Address

(Remarks made on formally taking office as Yale's 16th president, New Haven, October 6, 1950)

We are met here today to renew the life of an old and honorable institution. In a few months we shall celebrate our 250th anniversary. The "Collegiate School" founded at Parson Russel's house in Branford in 1701 has become a great university, the second oldest in the United States, the ninth oldest in the English-speaking world. Its fame has no national boundaries. The work of its scholars and teachers is known and respected in every quarter of the globe. In American higher education its prestige and influence are second to none. This is the trust we receive here today and that our presence here pledges us to maintain. It is a great responsibility, one that calls upon each of us for the best effort of which he is capable, and upon all of us for a common sense of the direction those efforts must take.

The times are not auspicious for learning. They are times of war, and war imposes a terrible burden of proof on everything that does not directly serve its ends. Just and noble as we believe those ends to be in our own case, war and the preparation for war are not conducive to the reflective life that produces great teaching and great scholarship. The teacher senses his remoteness from his fellow men. The scholar's thoughts stray to the battlefield. The Promethean secret of the atom breeds fear and suspicion in all our hearts, inclining us to dismiss the past, to dread the future, and to live in the present. There is indeed "no hiding place," no fortress, and no academic cloister from which we can escape the consequences of this latest knowledge we have wrested from the gods. It seeks us all out as indiscriminately as the Roman soldier who slew Archimedes in the siege of Syracuse, not knowing who his victim was or that the scientific knowledge that died with him would not be regained for nearly eighteen hundred years.

What price the scholar's life in times like these, or the university's, whose purpose is to foster that life? There have been moments in which we have all asked ourselves these questions, and at certain of those moments I, for one, have found no answers. Yet I wonder if we know our own strength. The briefest glance into history shows us that we are supported by powerful traditions—not symbols or legends, but vital forces with remarkable capacity for survival. I would cite three of these traditions this afternoon: the tradition of higher learning, the university tradition, and the tradition of American democracy. Any one of these should give us courage. The three together form a tower of strength.

I do not know who first questioned the value of the scholar's life: it may have been one of Socrates' disciples who watched his master drink the hemlock. Surely no calling has been so much questioned—and despaired of —since that memorable event; and just as surely none has contributed so much to western civilization. What is the nature of this calling? Archimedes might have come down to us as a military strategist on the strength of the wonderful engines he contrived for the defense of Syracuse. But, says Plutarch, "he possessed so high a spirit, so profound a soul, and such treasures of scientific knowledge, that though these inventions had now obtained for him the renown of more than human sagacity, he yet would not deign to leave behind him any writing on such subjects; but . . . placed his whole affection and ambition in those purer speculations where there can be no reference to the vulgar needs of life—studies whose superiority to all others is unquestioned, and in which the only doubt can be whether the beauty and grandeur of the subjects examined, or the precision and cogency of the methods and means of proof, most deserve our admiration." The scholar, says Emerson, is the "delegated intellect" of mankind. In the degenerate state he becomes a "mere thinker, or still worse, the parrot of other men's thinking. . . . In the right state he is Man Thinking." To whom else do we owe our progress from savagery? To whom else do we pin our hopes of ending our periodic reversions to savagery and putting our engines of destruction to creative use? If the scholars of the past had waited for auspicious times to do their work, I doubt that we should be assembled here today. If they should now wait for total war to produce total peace, I doubt that our successors will be assembled here to mark Yale's 300th anniversary.

The scholar has always had to contend with his times. As we follow him through history, how thin his lifeline appears! The dreamer, the questioner, the restless migrant between past and future, he is seldom at home in the present or with the practical men of his generation. The practical men of Athens put Socrates to death; of Rome forced Galileo to deny what he had seen through his telescope; of Berlin drove a whole generation of scholars into exile; of Moscow frightened another generation into false witnesses and quacks. Anglo-American history embraces no such violent extremes. Yet even British and American scholars have suffered from test oaths—as they once did in the early days of both Oxford and Yale and do now in California; from economic adversity, with them an occupational disease; and from corrosively utilitarian national philosophies of life.

Higher learning is innate in western civilization. Unorganized in the ancient world, it was carried on by individual Greek, Hebrew, and Roman scholars with such zeal and competence that it took European scholars a thousand years to catch up with their attainments. The phrase implies a parallel achievement. It was not. Medieval scholars rediscovered the works of the ancients and built on their foundations. Aristotle emerges as the intellectual colossus whose writings bridge the gap and restore continuity between the two civilizations. Far be it from me to pass critical judgment on these works. But I observe that they all possess this common significance: they represent a continuous effort to free the human mind from ignorance and superstition, a continuous voyage of discovery of the human imagination. The voyage is lonely, for great scholarship is an individual experience. Often it carries the voyager onto stormy seas. Yet no explorer ever felt its urge more powerfully than the true scholar feels it every morning of his life.

Since the revival of learning that ended the Dark Ages, the university tradition has strongly reinforced the tradition of higher learning. The university has been the scholar's home. In ways that point a fearful object lesson to us today, European civilization had been reduced nearly to their own level by the barbarians who destroyed the Roman Empire. Learning, even in its most elementary forms of reading and writing, had been almost totally destroyed, and very likely would have been but for a few monasteries and cathedral schools. These kept the spark alive so that when Mohammedan scholars from Spain restored to Europe the works of Greek philosophers, mathematicians, and physicians, and the Justinian code of law, there were at least a handful of Europeans capable of understanding them. Toward the end of the twelfth century, groups of masters and students banded themselves together to exploit this newly rediscovered wealth of learning, first at Bologna, then at Paris, then at Oxford and Cambridge, calling their organizations *studia generalia, universitates,* and finally universities. We are the lineal heirs of Paris and the two English universities.

Historians consider the universities the outstanding intellectual achievement of the Middle Ages and credit them with determining the whole course of contemporary culture and thought. With manuscripts scarce and printing still two hundred years away, the part the earliest ones played in the general diffusion of knowledge is impossible to exaggerate. But it is for their institutional character that we take notice of them here. They brought together the study of the liberal arts (grammar, rhetoric, logic, arithmetic, geometry, astronomy, and music) with the pursuit of higher education in special fields (medicine, theology, law, philosophy). Thus they both deepened and broadened the higher learning. They deepened it by bringing this combination within the experience of a single individual, and they broadened it by making the experience available to much greater numbers of individuals. They did not attempt to cover every field of learning. That is neither the proper meaning of the word university nor, I submit, the proper policy for it to suggest to us. A group of men devoted to learning on the highest plane of intellectual and moral integrity would be an even more accurate historical definition of a university than an institution combining higher education with the liberal arts. But it is in their institutional design that we most clearly perceive the interlocking of the higher learning and university traditions and with it Yale's identity with the medieval universities.

I have said that we were the heirs of Paris, Oxford, and Cambridge. This is true in a very literal sense, as Oxford was founded by a migration of scholars from Paris about 1170, Cambridge by a migration from Oxford in 1209, Harvard by a group of Cambridge graduates in 1636, and Yale by a group of Harvard graduates in 1701. But there is more than antiquity in this lineage. In our graduate and professional schools we continue to extend our knowledge and project our imagination to the farthest frontiers of learning and beyond. And in our college of liberal arts we continue to prepare students for service on those frontiers. The importance of our graduate and professional schools, in our own day and age, is obvious. We can imagine the chaos and retrogression that would ensue in the arts and sciences and the professions if these schools, and others like them, should close their doors. The importance of the liberal arts is, if anything, even greater. Not only are they stepping stones to the professions. Generations of students have found them the best preparation for the ordinary work of the world.

This is particularly true in a democracy. The liberal arts inform and enlighten the independent citizens of a democracy in the use of his own resources. Broadened in our modern curriculum to include a wide range of humanistic, scientific, and social studies, they appeal to the most varied and subtle combinations of taste. Yet their fundamental purpose lies, not in their specific content, but in their stimulus to the individual student's powers of reason, judgment, and imagination. In a democracy, which rests upon the freedom and responsibility of the individual, they give that individual vision. They enlarge his capacity for self-knowledge and expand his opportunities for self-improvement. In a technological society whose working week is steadily shrinking, they render more profitable and more enjoyable the purposes to which he may put his steadily increasing leisure time. Even by the supreme practical test of modern warfare they have been judged the apprenticeship of the most alert and resourceful soldiers. They are the wellsprings of a free society.

It is in this way that the American democratic tradition forms the *tripos* with the traditions of higher learning and the university. Europeans and Englishmen have used their universities to train their intellectual and political leaders. We have conceived a broader purpose for higher education. This purpose regards all education as a preparation for life, and higher education but the culminating phase of a process that should be available to all who have the capacity to partake of it. By capacity we do not mean merely intellectual competence. We mean intellectual competence tempered by character, judgment, and moral responsibility. Our purpose does not assume equal capacity or equal attainment among men. It holds, rather, that if men are to be thrown upon their own individual resources in society, society should prepare them for that responsibility and should not allow that preparation to be limited by anything other than the individual's innate ability to benefit by it. This was Jefferson's corollary to popular sovereignty, his key to equal opportunity and a truly mobile, democratic society. This was the means whereby the people could not only instruct themselves in the use of the franchise but also produce their leaders and teachers in every sphere of life. It was education in this sense that Jefferson called "the most legitimate engine of government" and of which he said, in words that stand out vividly against the Iron Curtain, "If a nation expects to be ignorant and free, in a state of civilization, it expects what never was and never will be."

From this third great tradition Yale derives great strength. For if democracy depends upon education as its "engine of government," the proper functioning of that engine depends upon the maintenance of standards; and in this work Yale stands, with a few—a very few—of her sister universities, *prima inter pares*. Twenty-nine million children go to school in the United States and 2,500,000 men and women to college. By 1960 our school population is expected to increase to 37,000,000 and our college to 4,600,000. Is this too much education? We might as well say there is too much health. Let us admit that under the weight of such numbers quality is bound to suffer; that the statistics cover a multitude of sins—underpaid and incompetent teachers, promising students neglected or allowed to fall by the wayside, others misdirected, others carried as supercargo beyond their proper destination, and an infinite variety of nature faking in the name of higher education. Let us say that relative to our resources—to what we could do if we wanted to—our American system of education varies as a company of infantry would vary if it went into action armed with everything from rockets to flintlocks. Still we can say that we have made the greatest effort to educate ourselves ever made by a free people, and that the hearts of our own people, and of every people in the world to whom it is given to know about it, are behind that effort.

How can we say that there is too much higher education when we think of it in these terms? Can we not afford it? We spend on higher education barely one quarter of what we spend on tobacco, less than we spend on barber and beauty shops. Yale's entire plant and endowment together would not pay for two battleships like the *Missouri*. If our total college population should double by 1960 it would not increase the amount we spend on higher education, even assuming full employment and the consequent loss of students to the labor market, to much more than 3 per cent of the total gross product of our economy.

To argue saturation in higher education is to claim perfection for hundreds of educational institutions (not excepting Yale) that are far from it. Or it is to assume a narrowly vocational purpose for higher education and discredit it by pointing to momentary gluts in this or that profession. Or to believe that every American with the requisite ability gets to college. Or that those who lack that ability are routed into other channels. If we believe that higher learning, as we have deepened and broadened it, is not only a necessary preparation for the professions but the best preparation for a full, useful, and enjoyable life in a free society, how can we deny it to any citizen who is both able and eager to assimilate it? Are the liberal arts irrelevant to a mechanic? In our modern society, his material rewards and his store of leisure time make him their natural beneficiary. No one is born to drudgery in a democracy, and if drudgery is thrust upon any of us (as it is in some form or other upon all of us) the liberal arts are its antidote. We are all voters and as such all equally in need of as much enlightenment as education can give us. As men and women living in a state of civilization, the lives and welfare of all of us are identified with Man Thinking.

These traditions give us courage for the future no matter how black it may look from day to day. These are the things Yale lives and works for, in war and peace. They are things to cherish and defend in times of war; to fight for, when there is fighting; and to return to when the fighting is over.

Survival Is Not Enough

(*An Atlantic Monthly article, April, 1951*)

Communist aggression in Asia has scored one tactical success not commonly recognized as such. It has struck a body blow at American higher education. Barely recovered from the disruptions of the second World War, our colleges and universities are once more called upon to sacrifice their students, faculties, and curricula to military necessity. No one knows how great these sacrifices may be: the colleges may be confronted with the worst financial crisis in their history. If the lives of many private institutions be threatened, our public institutions will suffer and our whole educational system will be the poorer. If the long-run objective of communism is to destroy our free society at its source, the farther we go toward stripping our colleges of students, dismissing their teachers, and "accelerating" their curricula, the nearer the Communists will have got to achieving that objective.

Such desperate measures can be justified in the name of national survival. We will fight to survive, and we will fight before our backs are to the wall, for our security and our principles. All this is clear in our history, our character, and our present actions. Our college students and professors share this destiny with their countrymen in every walk of life. They could not escape it if they wished to, and they do not wish to. But they have a mission in society, and the question is how much of that mission they can sacrifice without again "losing the peace" and perhaps even losing the war.

In the emergency, we talk of college education as a nonessential and an expendable. While we lavish our ingenuity and resources on the weapons of war, we neglect and even handicap the men who will use them. This is a high price to pay for survival. And what price survival if we become a headless monster?

Our colleges and universities are not ivory towers. They are wellsprings of humanistic and scientific learning and of the spirit that puts that learning to use in the cause of freedom. Their long-run value to our arts and sciences, to our whole ideal of a free society and a free culture, is hardly open to question.

And in the emergency? Never in the whole history of warfare has the strength of armies depended so much on their soldiers'—especially their officers'—articles of faith as it does today. What else has transformed the sleeping peasantry of Russia and China into great military machines? What has muffled the Voice of America and inhibited our efforts to preserve world peace but the impression we have given other people that, for all our wealth, generosity, and efficiency, we are "light half-believers in our casual creeds"? Cromwell's maxim, in obedience to which he made himself one of the world's great military geniuses, should be engraved on the walls of the Pentagon: "I had rather have a plain russet-coated captain that knows what he fights for, and loves what he knows, than that which you call a gentleman and is nothing else." The greatest source—greater than any other in our society and greater than all others put together—of American captains who know what they fight for and love what they know is our colleges and universities. The greatest, indeed the exclusive, source of the scientific learning and personnel necessary to sustain those captains in modern warfare is our colleges and universities. We tamper with that source at our peril. There is more identity between our long-run cultural interests and our short-run military interest than there is conflict.

How short will the short run be? Local "Korean" wars may continue indefinitely. The first frightful spasm of global war may resolve itself into an interminable war of the worlds. This is not a situation we can dispose of by dropping everything "for the duration" and picking up where we left off, as though we were knocking off for lunch. The only safe assumption is a long pull, and the only proper goal at the end of it is victory, not survival. We seek neither triumph nor conquest but a fulfillment of the moral purposes that moved us to make the effort in the first place. This must be a sustained effort. It cannot even begin if it counts the days and gambles on "the duration." The very nature of the effort places the highest premium we have ever placed upon our educational system. It rules out "education as usual," not for the reasons usually given but because education as usual is not good enough. It calls on us to educate not fewer citizens but more, not less well but better.

This is the greatest irony of all: that the circumstances calling for the greatest educational effort in our history should be so hostile to that effort. In 1948 President

Truman's Commission on Higher Education, declaring that "the future of our civilization depends on the direction education takes, not just in the distant future, but in the days immediately ahead," fixed our goal at a college population of 4,600,000 by 1960. This would have meant 2,500,000 men and women enrolled in the thirteenth and fourteenth grades, 1,500,000 in the fifteenth and sixteenth, and 600,000 above the sixteenth. Based on an inventory of our needs, resources, and native ability as reflected in Army General Classification Tests, this figure was given as the minimum necessary to fulfill our social ideals and maintain our economic and cultural progress. In addition to this quantitative responsibility, the commission charged our colleges and universities with qualitative improvements of all kinds, particularly those "which will make clear the ethical values and the concept of human relations upon which our political system rests."

The report of the commission makes wistful reading today. Out of a total college population of around 2,300,000, we now have about 1,500,000 men in our colleges and universities (grades thirteen through sixteen). Of these we expect to graduate approximately 380,000 this June. As these words are written, we are debating a military service law that would reduce the total male enrollment to 950,000 next year, 665,000 the year after, and 643,000 in 1954–55. If the law should be enacted, our graduating classes would drop proportionately from 380,000 this year to 81,000 in 1955. If the ratio of college men to women that obtained in 1940 be applied to the Truman Commission's goal, it would give us a total male enrollment (grades thirteen through sixteen) in 1960 of 2,400,000. The total predicted for 1960 if the present

Opposing precollege service are two serious considerations. The first is the interruption in the flow of doctors, engineers, and other scientific personnel, which many experts in these fields believe would be disastrous. This can be prevented by selecting students and assigning them to specialized college training after three or four months of basic military training. A more serious consideration is the maturity of high school graduates as compared with men who have completed at least one year of college. If the Cromwellian maxim is sound, the odds are in favor of the college men as against an army of schoolboys. The former should be a more stable, more resourceful, and more purposeful fighting force both in action and in training.

If the American high school took its students as far as its British or European counterparts, we might dismiss this consideration. But it does not. On the contrary, the graduate of a British public school or a French *lycée* is ready to enter our college sophomore year, and I have known some to enter our junior. It may be that the intellectual apparatus of these young men—particularly the Europeans—has been developed beyond their years. Nevertheless, they have had better discipline and, by definition, more higher education than our high school graduates. The Russian military service law now in force defers high school students until they graduate or reach the age of 20—the level of our college sophomores. The basic assumption underlying this whole discussion is that we are in for a long pull, in which we stand to win or lose, not only as soldiers but as representatives of a particular civilization. To send our young men abroad in either capacity before they fully comprehend that mission is to neglect one of the most essential phases of their training.

On the whole, with more than a million men becoming 18 each year, I think we can leave the choice of military service before or after entering college with those whose ages permit them to exercise it. Some will prefer to get it over with at once, others to take a year of college. The more freedom of choice we can preserve in these Spartan times the better. But we have no choice whatsoever in what we must do for these young men. Whether they are called at 18 or 18½ or 19, as high school graduates or as college freshmen, we must give them the richest educational experience of which we are capable before they go, and the greatest educational opportunities of which we are capable when they come back. Only thus can we put in the field an army that knows what it fights for and loves what it knows, the present soldiers and the future scholars.

This is the prime responsibility of American higher education in the emergency. Apart from preserving the higher learning that for two thousand years has instructed and illuminated western civilization, apart from the scientific research that may hold our lives and our national security in the balance, alone and distinct and urgent, is the intellectual and spiritual fate of the men of fighting age today who will be tomorrow's philosophers and statesmen. They are our best hope of survival. What do we propose to do for them?

One of the first answers on everyone's lips is "acceleration." In the terms in which it is generally understood, I think this is a poor answer. These terms contemplate a round-the-clock, three-term cycle that crowds four normal academic years into less than three calendar years and keeps on revolving until the faculty collapses, the students revolt, or the emergency ends, with the odds favoring the demise of the faculty. Here we have another expression of our naïveté as to the nature and purpose of education. Our colleges and universities may be driven to accelerate by financial necessity, by the terms of our military service law, by ROTC contracts or some other *force majeure*. I do not know a single member of the teaching profession who has anything good to say for it on its merits. Our purpose is not to save our students from the draft, or salvage their tuitions, or get them as far as we can up the four-year ladder before they are called to duty. Our purpose is to give them a sense of what they are fighting for, a mature introduction to the higher learning of their civilization in the fullness of its humanistic wisdom and scientific genius, and a desire that will survive the drudgery of military service to come back and carry that civilization forward.

We cannot accomplish this purpose by accelerating. I think we would come nearer to it if we gave our students fewer courses and let them take their time with their studies. When I described acceleration recently to a distinguished French colleague, a member of the Collège de France whose ancestors have been teachers since the eighteenth century, he shook his head sadly and said: "Knowledge without culture. Knowledge without pleasure. Absorption without digestion." "Followed by regurgitation," I prompted. "I hope so," he replied; "that at least would show that the students were healthy." To keep our fields fertile we practice crop rotation. Shall we do less for our minds? To speed up our basic courses in the arts and sciences for this long-drawn time of trouble promises nothing but intellectual erosion and academic dust bowls. No one suggests that we take our summers off to loaf. Our faculties need them for the research and writing that sustains their teaching through the academic year. To our self-supporting students (a great majority in the nation) they are an economic necessity. Our ROTC units might use them to intensify both the course work and outdoor training which they have to conduct at a minimum during the academic year. Students deferred for specialized nonmilitary training could make similar use of them. For these two groups, for students not yet called up, and ultimately for those returning from service, I would be willing to compromise on an eight-week summer term of intensive work in such subjects (for example, foreign languages or elementary mathematics) as lend themselves to intensive treatment and afford a contrast with the regular term's work. But as a matter of principle I would far rather award a B.A. degree for three rich, unhurried years than for four lean ones run off against a stop watch.

In the long run it may be necessary to shorten the time consumed in the eight grades of high school and college. If students have to budget two or more years to military service they may very well become impatient with the four-year college curriculum. I do not see why we should not make it possible for them to earn their B.A. degrees in three years, whether consecutive or interrupted by military service. But there is one fundamental condition precedent. To accomplish this purpose, without cheapening the B.A., means jacking up our standards of secondary education. We cannot give a three-year B.A. to students who are inadequately prepared for it. Even with the four-year degree, as every college admissions office knows, our secondary school performance is very uneven in this respect. At the best our secondary schools are as good as any in the world, and with a few curricular extensions and revisions could easily carry their students as far as any. At the worst their students are ill-prepared for a four-year B.A., and the worst greatly depresses the average. The result is that the best trained students mark time as college freshmen while their less favored classmates catch up, and they all enter sophomore year from scratch. To "accelerate" by eliminating this redundancy and waste motion would accomplish an educational reform long overdue in the United States. The emergency gives us a powerful incentive to attempt it.

The only reason why the "worst" American secondary schools should not be as good as the best is our indifference, our failure to comprehend the purpose of education. This is what tolerates the politics, incompetence, and miserably inadequate teachers' salaries that prolong the adolescence of the American youth and send him off to college with a child's mind in a man's body. Here is an area of "war effort" in which our colleges and universities could cooperate with our secondary schools to the mutual advantage of both and the incalculable advantage of the nation. Here, conceivably, is a mission for our college teachers temporarily unemployed by military service legislation. Matching grants of public and private funds in support of this mission, properly defined and administered, would be a direct investment in the future of our political institutions and our culture.

There are many things our colleges and universities might do to improve the educational advantages of the men going off to war and the opportunities awaiting them on their return. They could run pilot plants to test and perfect the curricula of our twelfth and thirteenth grades, an experiment that might offer immediate benefits to the students and colleges concerned and have far-reaching consequences for our entire educational system. It would almost surely reveal more effective methods of accelerating—that is, by eliminating waste and treating boys like men instead of men like boys—than trying to pour four quarts into a three-quart bottle. They, the colleges and universities—both on their own and in cooperation with the United States Armed Forces Institute—might offer extension courses for men on military service. This might have many advantages. It would keep track of students who had left after a year of college. It would help sustain their momentum. It might enable them to anticipate a course or two. At the very least it would offer an improvement on the army's educational comics. Both projects—the pilot plants and the extension courses—would have the practical advantages of providing employment for the faculty and income for the college.

This is a time for self-inspection and self-improvement, for which opportunities exist on every campus. Far be it from me to say what others should do: I am too busy with the mote in my own eye. But I seem to see a country which wants better of its educational system, and deserves better of it, than it gets. Wherefore the discrepancy? Because—and here I return to my theme—we do not understand its purpose. We still think of it as a luxury and a privilege, when in reality it is a necessity and an obligation. We still (too often and too many of us) confuse it with other things, with politics, with business, with athletic sports. Once we see it clearly, how it all hangs together, from the primary school to the graduate school, and serves its purpose, in Jefferson's phrase, as "the most legitimate engine of government," I am convinced that we will speedily find ways for higher education to serve us in the emergency. We will find ways to rescue our colleges and universities from their financial difficulties and enlist them in the common cause. To doubt our ability to afford this is to doubt our reason. In 1947, the year of the Truman Commission's report, we spent $1,005,000,000 on higher education in the United States. Last year we spent slightly over $1,000,000,000 on television sets. Five years ago nobody owned a television set. This is brand-new money, spent on a new toy, having nothing to do with the emergency, our security, or our survival, but only with our pleasure. It tends to prove —does it not?—that we can always find the money for what we want if we want it badly enough.

I would argue from this that we can easily afford to finance our mixed system of public and private higher education as an essential industry in the emergency and an essential key to the survival and progress of our civilization. But the will must precede the plans. That is why I would say to the planners and accelerators what Thoreau urged his preacher to say to his well-intentioned, nervous, action-starved, news-hungry neighbors: "Pause! Avast! Why so seeming fast, but deadly slow?"

Baccalaureate Address

(*First sermon to a Yale graduating class, New Haven, June 10, 1951*)

"Ye are the salt of the earth: but if the salt have lost his savour, wherewith shall it be salted?"

MATTHEW 5:13

If I divine the mood of you who are leaving Yale this spring, it is one of cheerful resignation. To your cheerfulness in all winds and weathers, in clear skies and at ceiling zero, we who have lived and worked among you are admiring witnesses. We take courage from your courage. But I observe also that you share the prevailing mood of the hour, which in your case consists of 960 bargains privately struck with fate—on fate's terms. I observe that you are resigned to a world in which people become numbers on Selective Service and Social Security cards; in which lotteries are illegal except when they deal with human life; and in which the individual, sacred to both Christianity and democracy, sometimes seems to exercise about as much control over his own fortunes and those of his fellow men as a baseball in the World Series.

I will say this much for your mood: at least it is healthier than the one which attended my own commencement. We were graduated into the greatest economic depression in history and the origins of the greatest war in history with assurances that poverty was about to be banished from the earth and that war had been outlawed among the nations. No such disillusionment lies in store for you as awaited us in 1929: come what may you are better prepared for it. But that is all I will say for your mood. As a philosophy of life it is as false in its fatalism as our mood was in its romanticism.

We have not resigned from the human race. Neither science nor technology nor all the deterministic doctrine inspired by them, nor the despotisms that have tried to force that doctrine upon mankind, have succeeded in producing a world that can function without our individual powers of reason, imagination, and conscience. We are not mere sponges or plankton afloat on a tide of causation over which we have no control. We are rational beings, capable of charting the tide, and navigating it, and even diverting and directing it. The salt—to return to the Bible's metaphor—has not lost its savor; and there would be no way of salting the earth if it had. There is no dialectical or technological substitute for the creative individual.

Whence come our doubts and hallucinations to the contrary? Partly from fear, partly from laziness. We are afraid that where, as in Soviet Russia, there is mystery there is also magic; that the Russians have possessed themselves of some supernatural means of enslaving the will of men; that they will blow us all to bits by methods unknown to western science. We have beguiled ourselves with gadgets, with machines that work for us, and think for us, and entertain us, and (as we believe in our folly) educate us, until our God-given individual powers have become atrophied through disuse. In this hypnotic state we have fallen prey to some of the very teachings we profess to abhor, the teachings of those who proclaim the world machine blueprinted in the Kremlin and the atomizing of the human race without the assistance of the bomb.

The last World War and the terrible weapons now in existence give us abundant reason to fear the next; and the ruthless and aggressive tactics of the Kremlin around the world give us every reason to think that the Russians are willing to gamble on it. But there is no reason in the unreasoning dread that exalts them into supermen and credits their doctrines with wonder-working properties. And as for the television sets that take us from our books, the business machines that clatter away under wall mottos reading "THINK," the electrical examination correctors that dispense with writing, the inner-spring mattresses that end up in bed boards, and the prefabricated knowledge that ends in remedial reading—for all this childish fascination with gadgetry we have only childishness as an excuse. Shall we then offer fear and childishness as proof that the individual has played out his role—that the salt has lost its savor?

No, you will say, but what about science and the industrial revolution now projecting itself into the atomic age? And I will answer you with the fact that whereas the first social interpreters of these phenomena were responsible for the idea of the submergence of the individual, modern scientists are the leaders in repudiating it.

I do not know what it is that makes each generation so

sure that its own set of circumstances is unique and yet forms a basis for universal preachments and predictions. The Bible says it is the essential vanity of man. I should say it is his innocence of history, of the cumulative experience of his fellow men. We are forever calculating our prospects on the strength of a mere peep through a knothole at this experience. So early economists who observed the first sensational progress of the industrial revolution deduced their concept of economic man, which the scientific socialists appropriated and developed into the full-blown doctrine of economic determination. The whole dialectical process is barely a hundred years old, and the leading figure in it was Karl Marx.

Let us concede that Marx chose an exceptional knothole—the British Museum—that he brought to it an exceptional intellectual apparatus, and that he kept his eye to it (day after day for nearly thirty-five years) with exceptional perseverance. His range of vision was still exceptionally limited. Man made his debut on the planet in the Pleistocene epoch of the Cenozoic era, about a million years ago. From the time he took up farming, in the Neolithic age, about 7000 B.C., his experiences have been relevant to modern economic society. There is every reason to extend this perspective to 7000 A.D., if not to 1,000,000 A.D. Marx's focal depth included little more than a bookish version of the industrial revolution in England between the years 1820 and 1860, with the preponderance of his evidence drawn from the earlier rather than the later part of that period. That is to say, Marx took as the verification of his hypothesis a static view of conditions in one country, already undergoing change while he wrote, and offered it to the world as both timeless and universal. Nor was his view entirely objective.

Marx was a bitter, vindictive, unhappy man, suffering the plagues of Job without Job's faith, tortured by poverty and disease, living in squalor, so proud and thin-skinned, as one of his most brilliant biographers tells us, that he made excessive demands on the world and when these were not satisfied (as they nearly always were not) turned in upon himself "in paroxysms of hatred and of rage." Yet it is this static, myopic, misanthropic view of human experience that is offered as the principal foundation for the belief that the machine is all and the individual is nothing, and for the Communist dictatorship that exploits that belief to suit its purposes. It has all the eerie aspects of those prehistoric Siberian mammoths frozen into the ice with hair and flesh intact, with everything, that is, except life and sense.

One would think that the very nature of Marx's vision would make it suspect; that the influence of his own baleful personality contradicted his own thesis; that the direct, personal influence of Lenin on the outcome of the Russian revolution (suppose the German High Command had never let him cross Germany in that sealed-up boxcar) contradicted it even more emphatically; and that the fact that the thesis has to be maintained by tyranny and enforced by secret police contradicted it finally and flatly. Still there remains our awe of science and the technology of our own time. What do our own observations tell us?

If we carry them far enough to include the opinions of modern scientists, they will tell us of steadily broadening horizons for the creative individual and of the urgent need for him to press on toward those horizons. "Man has risen, not fallen," writes George Gaylord Simpson in *The Meaning of Evolution.* "He can choose to develop his capacities as the highest animal and try to rise still further, or he can choose otherwise. The choice is his responsibility, and his alone. There is no automism that will carry him upward without choice or effort and there is no trend solely in the right direction. Evolution has no purpose; man must supply this for himself." To do so, to make the wise choice for himself and his fellow men is the ethical responsibility of man which he must discharge as an individual if he is ever going to realize its benefits as a species.

But, we say, can we not entrust this responsibility to others, to the elaborate teams of specialists that are constantly producing new techniques, new tools and, may we not assume, new visions of wisdom and justice? What do the scientists say to this? I suppose there is no more impressive example of team work in human history than that which produced the atomic bomb. Listen to the opinion of one of the world's outstanding scholars in that field, Percy Bridgman, whose researches in nuclear physics won him the Nobel Prize in 1946. So elaborate has the organization, equipment, and administrative detail become, writes Professor Bridgman, that each team of physicists "has to be driven by some one at the head who has the ideas. There is danger here that all the rest of the team will pick the brains of one man, with an ultimate decrease in the number of physicists in the community capable of independent and critical thought." And he goes on to say:

"The participation of the individual is necessary in every process of intelligence, not merely in the processes of science. Intelligence can be given a meaning only in terms of the individual. It seems to me that this has a far-reaching significance not usually appreciated, for I believe that here is to be found perhaps the most compelling justification for democracy. Intelligence is based on the individual. An authoritarian society in which the individual is suppressed cannot, by the nature of intelligence, be characterized by *general* intelligence." *

Gentlemen of the graduating class: this is a truth Christ perceived and most surely intended to communicate to his disciples when he told them they were the salt of the earth for which there was no substitute; and that they were the light of the world, but they must not hide that light under a bushel. This is also the truth that the founders of this Republic perceived and Jefferson proclaimed when he said that morality, compassion, and generosity were innate elements of the human constitution, capable of cultivation in individuals, and capable of transmission to society through individuals. It is for life in this free, Christian society that we have prepared you at Yale. It remains for you, each according to his talents and each as an individual, to embody the degree of wisdom and integrity we may expect from that society.

* *Isis, 37,* Pts. 3 and 4, nos. 109, 110.

250th Anniversary Celebration Address

(Remarks at the convocation held at New Haven, October 19, 1951)

I have the honor to convoke this meeting in commemoration of the founding of the Collegiate School which became Yale University and to present to you the representatives, here assembled, of the forty-one colleges and universities founded or first administered by Yale graduates. I also have the honor to present the representatives of the three universities from which we trace our descent: Oxford, Cambridge, and Harvard.

Two hundred and fifty years ago this fall there took place in this Commonwealth the events which we celebrate here today. Tradition has it that in the month of September 1701 ten Connecticut Congregational ministers foregathered in the home of the Reverend Samuel Russel in Branford and there made a gift of books "for the founding of a College in this colony." History antedates tradition in ascribing their purpose to John Davenport of Coventry, Warwickshire, and either Brasenose or Magdalen College, Oxford, who in 1638 founded the New Haven Colony and throughout his life strove to grace it with a college. And history records the fulfillment of their purpose on October 9, 1701, when there was passed in New Haven, by the General Assembly of His Majesty King William III's Colony of Connecticut, "An Act for Liberty to erect a Collegiate School," wherein "Youth may be instructed in the Arts & Sciences who through the blessing of Almighty God may be fitted for Publick employment both in Church & Civil State."

By virtue of this Act the ten founders became the first trustees of what is now Yale University. They established their Collegiate School at Saybrook, elected one of their number, the Reverend Abraham Pierson, rector, and in March 1702 enrolled their first student. In 1716 they voted to move the School to New Haven, which had outbid all other communities in the Colony in hospitality, land, and money, and two years later, out of gratitude to the Honorable Elihu Yale of New England, Madras, and London, for his gift of nine bales of goods, they christened it Yale College.

It is fitting on this occasion to remember the ten Connecticut ministers whose work survives in Yale University. They were James Noyes of Stonington; Israel Chauncey of Stratford; Thomas Buckingham of Saybrook; Abraham Pierson of Killingworth; Samuel Mather of Windsor; Samuel Andrew of Milford; Timothy Woodbridge of Hartford; James Pierpont of New Haven; Noadiah Russel of Middletown; and Joseph Webb of Fairfield. All but one had been born in New England, and all but one were graduates of Harvard. Thus they renewed, on American soil, the purpose that had been transplanted to it by the graduates of the ancient English universities who founded Harvard, as we have renewed it since their time, through our own graduates, to the institutions of learning represented here today.

It would be reading too much into history to find in that purpose, as it expressed itself in Branford and New Haven in 1701, the full-blown concept of the modern university. But we need not torture history to find the essence. Nothing is so revealing of this essence as the simple words of our charter, identifying the welfare of both church and state with the study of the arts and sciences. The cultural heritage embodied in the liberal arts is here blended with the piety of contemporary Puritanism and the emerging, free, self-governing democracy of the future.

The graduates of the English universities who founded Harvard, and the graduates of Harvard who founded Yale, brought to us a living shoot from the tree of learning whose roots reach down through western culture to the lore and learning of ancient Greece. The piety of the Puritan revolution which here and there had miscarried into narrow sectarianism as it would continue to do, from time to time, in the future, did not stifle this growth. On the whole, it stimulated it. For that piety was but the moral, at times mystical, aspect of a way of life whose slogan was "the priesthood of all believers" and whose aim was the freedom of the human intelligence and the human conscience from all dogmas and tyrannies. The founders' respect for learning speaks for itself: the scholar rubs elbows with the moralist. Both share the natural piety, the simple moral earnestness that for all our shortcomings has pervaded our culture and extended the aims of American higher education beyond the mere cultivation of the intellect to the preparation for life in a free society and the discovery and fulfillment of man's ultimate purpose in the universe. These aims are well represented here today by an honorable company of colleges and universities sharing with us in an honorable tradition.

We cannot, I repeat, claim all of this enlightened dispensation for the founders of the Collegiate School assembled in Parson Russel's house last month two hundred and fifty years ago, nor for the General Assembly of the Colony of Connecticut that met ten days ago in the same year. We must read it implicitly in the writings of John Davenport. But we may fairly hold these men responsible for thinking, writing, and acting as they did, and give them as we do in this company, some honor for having done so.

New York Herald Tribune
Forum Address

(Keynote address delivered at the 20th annual Forum, "Balancing Moral Responsibility and Scientific Progress," New York, October 22, 1951)

With the opening of this Forum we renew man's immemorial effort to find his place as an individual in a world that seems to recognize him only as a species. Since that moment, lost in the mists of time, when man first looked upon himself and saw the image of God, he has struggled against all the powers of nature and the supernatural, and against all the tyrannies of his fellow men, to fulfill the promise in that image. He has lived to the full, in pleasure and pain, the gregarious life to which half of his instincts and appetites committed him. And, in response to the other half, he has striven in every element on earth, in the skies above the earth, and in the waters under the earth, to express himself as an individual.

Philosophers have long recognized this centrifugal conflict in the bosom of man, and we, like every generation before us, have been witnesses to its political manifestations. Our world is divided between political philosophies proclaiming man's mechanistic fate as a species and those which proclaim his creative destiny as an individual. At the moment the mechanistic idea seems to be in the ascendant. It is propagated at the point of the sword by dictatorships now governing nearly half the peoples of the world and seeking to extend their dominion over the rest. It is given credence among the free peoples either because of their poverty, which depresses them, or because of their secret weapons and their automatic machines, which mystify and baffle them. Never in history, or so it seems to us, has the individual defended his birthright against such formidable odds.

This is a dark outlook for a country like ours which by tradition and temperament looks to the individual for the salvation of the race. We may be thankful that it is only an outlook and not a reality. For the mood that exalts the machine (and fills the waiting rooms of our psychiatrists) is an aberration. We do not know our strength; and we do not know our strength because we do not know our history. Time and again we have seen the individual apparently ready to exit from the stage only to have him change his mind, or to return, with fresh and more dynamic lines and a whole new development of the plot. We had communism in the Plymouth Colony in 1620, two centuries before Marx wrote his *Manifesto* and three centuries before the Russians ever heard of it, and gave it up, after a pragmatic test, because, as Governor Bradford wrote in his diary,

> The experience that was had in this commone course and condition, tried sundry years, and that

> amongst godly and sober men, may well evince the vanities of that conceite of Platos and other ancients, applauded by some of later times;—that the taking away of propertie, and bringing in communitie into a comone wealth, would make them happy and florishing; as if they were wiser then God. For this comunitie (so farr as it was) was found to breed much confusion and discontent, and retard much imployment that would have been to their benefite and comforte.

We had totalitarianism, complete with purges and secret police, in the Massachusetts Bay Colony, three centuries before Hitler, Stalin, and Mussolini; we gave it up in revulsion, and drafted statutes and constitutions to prevent its recurrence in the future.

In our traffic with foreign nations we have always looked out on a world full of despotisms. When was it ever not so? As colonies we were their pawns. As a young republic we were surrounded by them, and if the airplane had been invented a century earlier than it actually was invented, the chances are we would still be their pawn. Democracy is a very new thing in the world. Our knowledge of man in society goes back to the Neolithic age, nine thousand years ago. Over that span of time man has seen and suffered despotisms of every conceivable variety. We follow their rise and fall in the pages of Toynbee and read their epitaph in Shelley's poem, "Ozymandias":

> I met a traveller from an antique land
> Who said: Two vast and trunkless legs of stone
> Stand in the desert. Near them, on the sand,
> Half sunk, a shattered visage lies, whose frown,

And wrinkled lip, and sneer of cold command,
Tell that its sculptor well those passions read
Which yet survive, stamped on these lifeless things,
The hand that mocked them, and the heart that fed:
And on the pedestal these words appear:
"My name is Ozymandias, king of kings:
Look on my works, ye Mighty, and despair!"
Nothing beside remains. Round the decay
Of that colossal wreck, boundless and bare
The lone and level sands stretch far away.

Democracy, the hopeful philosophy, attuned to man's instincts as an individual and addressed to their cultivation for the benefit of society, first appeared in Athens about 500 B.C., saw fitful revival in the Italian city states of the eleventh and twelfth centuries A.D., and later in the Swiss cantons, but did not make its modern appearance until the Puritan revolution in England in the middle years of the seventeenth century. It did not attain the form in which we know it until the nineteenth century. Compared with despotism it is but a few minutes old. The remarkable fact is not that it is still opposed by despotism but that it has survived that opposition as vigorously as it has.

It has survived because time and again it has proved, under stress, its ability to harmonize and make productive in every sphere of thought and action the individual and the social instincts innate in man. In these respects it has demonstrated its superiority over all other political philosophies. All try to draw the line between the opportunities and responsibilities of the individual and those of society, but none draws it so subtly in accordance with reality as democracy. And what is that reality? It is that for nine thousand years society has depended upon its members as individuals for those creative achievements of mind and spirit that have guided it along the path of civilization. The spark from heaven falls. Who picks it up? The crowd? Never. The individual? Always. It is he and he alone, as artist, inventor, explorer, scholar, scientist, spiritual leader, or statesman, who stands nearest to the source of life and transmits its essence to his fellow men. Let them tie his hands or stop his mouth or dragoon him in the name of uniformity, and they cut themselves off from that source in equal measure.

Wisdom and virtue cannot be forced from a crowd as eggs are from chickens under electric lights. There is no such thing as general intelligence. There is only individual intelligence communicating itself to other individual intelligences. And there is no such thing as public morality, there is only a composite of private morality. The Athenian statesman Pericles perceived these truths when he said of democracy in its earliest phase that it trusted "less in system and policy than to the native spirit of our citizens." And so did Thomas Jefferson, on the threshold of our own age, when he wrote, "It is the manners and spirit of a people which preserve a republic in vigor." The same could be said of all forms of government, but of none so truly as that in which the voice of the people is the voice of God.

This is another way of saying, is it not, that democracy is fundamentally a moral philosophy, a fact which, more than any other in its nature and history, has enabled it to survive all of its previous incarnations. This is as true now in the atomic age as it was in the age of Pericles. It is a truth whose consequences will be read when archaeologists dig up the remains of our civilization. If they there find images like Shelley's Ozymandias it will be because we have failed to cultivate our powers at the source. We have the means for this in the most far-reaching system of education any free people has ever known, a system created and developed expressly for this purpose. We have the material resources to enable this system to fulfill its purpose without diverting a penny from the essential needs of our armed forces or from any other national interest of comparable importance. The problem is to create the will.

In the solution of this problem hangs the fate of our nation and our civilization. For the very scientific progress that some think spells the doom of democracy depends for its vitality on two things: first, the continuing discoveries of individuals in the realm of pure science, hence the continuing educational process that produces those individuals; and second, a social philosophy that converts the human energy newly rescued from drudgery by technological advances to uses consistent with this purpose. This vast store of energy, exceeding in human terms our greatest accomplishment in the conservation of natural resources, in military and political terms equivalent to the enlistment of a powerful new ally in the defense of democracy, is at hand and ready to use. How shall we use it? Shall we abandon it to the entertainment industry? Shall we neglect it while we accuse one another of treason, like the farmer in the Bible who spent so much time pulling up tares he harvested no ripe wheat? Shall we forget it in our fear of the ideas of a group of Russian doctrinaires, isolated even from their own people, whose conception of the world is not as sound as Columbus' nor as courageous as Ferdinand and Isabella's? If we do these things we shall have to answer for them just as surely as the broken statue of Ozymandias in the Egyptian desert answers for all bodies politic that hold their individual members in contempt. For "Every tree that bringeth not forth good fruit is hewn down, and cast into the fire."

Report to the Alumni, 1950-51

(First report as president, November, 1951)

Fifty-one years ago almost to the day, President Hadley opened the report of his first year in office as follows:

"The recent growth of Yale has been so rapid, not only in numbers and endowment, but in the variety of interests involved, that a President's Report can no longer give that detailed account of the events of the year which was possible a short time ago."

If this was true in 1900, it is true with another half century's vengeance today. In 1900 Yale had a total student enrollment of 2,542 and a faculty of 265. In 1950–51, having declined from a postwar peak of 9,017, our student body numbered 7,745 and our faculty 1,505.* Our budget for 1951 was nearly four times as large as our endowment of 1900. And the "variety of interests involved" has grown proportionately, in both number and complexity.

The educational and administrative affairs of the University can indeed no longer be treated comprehensively

* Both 1900 and 1950–51 faculty figures include full-time and part-time teachers, and research associates and assistants.

in a president's report, and such is not the purpose of this one. Its purpose is, rather, to sketch to the alumni Yale's place in the world as it appeared from Woodbridge Hall in the first year of the Korean war—to take stock of the position to which we have attained in our two hundred and fifty years and of the outstanding problem we must solve if we are to maintain that position.

There is good reason, I think, for placing this much emphasis on affairs outside the University. Not only do they contain (and obscure) the answers to most of the practical questions submitted to me in the sixty-odd reports of the educational and administrative officers of the University. They present, in the aggregate, one vital, all-embracing question that must be faced by the entire Yale community; namely, how can we fulfill our responsibilities and realize our objectives as a private university in an age of steadily expanding public enterprise and protracted war?

In stating the question thus, I do not imply any fundamental conflict or cross purposes between public and private education in the United States. On the contrary, I think that as Americans we may all take pride in the fact that the founders of our country recognized the education of its citizens as a national necessity and a public responsibility. It has always been to our common interest (and never more so than at present) that as many of us receive as good an education as possible; and this has always imposed a burden on our economy far heavier than our private resources could bear. The predicted enrollment of our primary and secondary schools for the present academic year is 35,000,000, and of our colleges 2,225,000. The great weight of this burden must, of necessity, be borne by our public institutions. It is to our interest as Yale graduates that the graduates of these public institutions, our friends and associates in every walk of life, in every profession, and on every level of responsibility, receive the best education of which they are capable; it is to their interest that Yale should continue to exist, and to prosper, as a private institution.

I do not argue the case for private enterprise in higher education in Yale's interest but in the national interest. If we believe that a society in which authority is diffused and individual enterprise flourishes is preferable to one that is centralized and regimented on the totalitarian pattern; if we believe that within the society of our choice there are certain dominions of the human soul and the human mind in which the state trespasses at everyone's, including its own, ultimate peril; if we believe these fundamental articles of American democracy, then I think the welfare of Yale as a private institution of higher learning requires no special pleading; and I venture the opinion that our friends and colleagues in the public institutions are as solicitous of this welfare as our own alumni. That is why I put the question as I have: not how can we merely survive on private terms, but how can we continue as a private institution to render the service the nation deserves and expects of us. Unless we recognize the importance of that question and apply ourselves to its solution with great wisdom and singleness of purpose, our future will be in doubt. By the Yale community I mean every undergraduate and graduate student, faculty member, and alumnus; and by recognizing the importance of the question I mean being able to perceive its relationship to every other question within our respective spheres of interest no matter how pressing these may seem at the moment. This, I submit, is the first and most urgent need of Yale, and I have therefore made it the principal subject of this report.

At the conclusion of his administration, President Seymour could give a good account of Yale. He could faithfully report that the scholarly prestige of our faculty was at its peak, that the vast majority of our departments of instruction ranked "among the very first in the nation," that our student body was second to none, and that (with exceptions which I shall mention) our resources for scholarly research were in general unexcelled and in some cases unequaled. This meant that, with the perversion of higher education in Russia, the disasters it had suffered in Europe, and the role of leadership now entrusted to the United States in world affairs, Yale had assumed universal responsibilities of great consequence. As I pointed out in my inaugural address, it meant that we, together with a very few other American, British, and European universities, had assumed educational leadership of the free nations.

Our mission was clear. It was to carry on the search for the ultimate truths concerning man and his place in the universe that had begun with the ancient Greeks and had guided and inspired our civilization ever since their day. We must preserve the results of this search, through teaching, and press it forward with constantly renewed vigor, through research; and we must maintain in the combined process the highest standards of which our society is capable. In one degree or another every school, college, and university in the United States and the free nations associated with it stood to lose or benefit by the way we acquitted ourselves in this mission. To fulfill it would be to contribute most powerfully to the preservation of our civilization. To fail in it, in an age that puts a steadily increasing burden of proof on all private enterprise, would mean at the least forfeiting our leadership and with it, in all probability, our status as a private institution; and at the worst, sharing in the responsibility for a new and worse Dark Age. What were our chances?

On June 25, just five days before I assumed office, the North Koreans launched what then seemed—and yet might prove—the opening encounter of the third World War. The effects of this aggressive action, which forced us back into large-scale mobilization for an unpredictable period, were immediately felt by our colleges and universities. Barely recovered from the upheaval of the second World War, their student bodies just returning to compassable size and their faculties to productive teaching and scholarship, they were now threatened with the disruption of their proper functions and activities for the second time within a decade.

There was no denying the magnitude of the world crisis and the peril to national security that seemed to require a repetition of these sacrifices. Nor had we any inclination to shirk our duty. On the contrary, we immediately volunteered as much of our resources as might be useful in the defense effort. We granted leave to members of our faculty holding reserve commissions and for special service in the government. And in company with the virtually unanimous membership of the Association of American Universities, we went on record in favor of universal military service and training. In line with these policies, we undertook certain strategic research and specialized training for the armed forces, agreed to expand to the limit our facilities for reserve officer training, and as late as April, before the present selective service policy was clarified, were tightening our belts for reductions in our undergraduate enrollment of as much as 40 per cent. These were minimal provisions against the worst that we all feared might happen.

At the same time there could be no denying the serious consequences, to the country as well as to the colleges, of another major interruption in higher education. The immediate consequences soon became apparent in shortages of doctors, engineers, and other scientifically trained personnel required both by the armed forces and by the war economy necessary to support them. Of less immediate but potentially even greater concern were the compounded deficits in the skills and professions responsible for our cultural development; the specific deficit of teachers adequate in both number and quality to the desperate needs of our public schools; the whole break in the continuity of higher learning, so vital a process in the development of our civilization and so urgent a need of any nation chosen by fate to organize and lead the defense of that civilization. I have discussed these consequences elsewhere and will not labor them here. The irony of a situation that called on higher education for the greatest effort in its history and at the same time placed seemingly insurmountable obstacles in its way speaks for itself.

The return to mobilization gave a new impetus to the expansion of public enterprise, which requires no documentation here. It is important, however, that we appreciate the extent to which this has affected higher education even in our part of the world. European universities have long been state controlled. That is why so few of them offered any effective resistance to dictatorship. In Great Britain, where their independence of governmental or any other form of outside control has been greater than anywhere else in the world, they are now dependent upon the government for approximately two-thirds of their annual income. Although they are confident that this will not compromise their traditional independence, it remains to be seen how it will stand the test of time. What few of us realize is that in our own country, where public and private education have flourished side by side for nearly two centuries, the trend is similar. In 1900 barely 10 per cent of our total annual expenditures on higher education in the United States was public in origin. Today the proportion is about 50 per cent, and is increasing steadily. While a small proportion of this public money finds its way into the private institutions and a somewhat larger proportion of the private money into the public, the main stream of each stays on its own side of the watershed.

The results of this flow for the 1,056 universities, colleges, and professional schools in existence in the United States in 1948 were as follows:

	Public	*Private*
Number of institutions	159	897
Enrollment	977,400	1,242,000
Income	$863,000,000	$923,000,000

In other words, while the funds were not so unevenly divided in relation to numbers of students, the one-seventh of the institutions that were public received nearly half the total income, while the six-sevenths of them that were private split the other half. It is obvious, is it not, that we cannot be content with our statistical average in this latter half if we are to carry out our mission as standard-bearer. Our statistical average would give us an income of just over $1,000,000. Our budget for last year was $17,000,000, and this was an economy budget representing hopes deferred and responsibilities unfulfilled. Among a group of institutions competing for available financial resources at odds of 7 to 1 against them, we are attempting to maintain a working advantage of more than 17 to 1 in our favor.

A comparison of the sources of our income with the national average and the average for private institutions will show how we have managed to keep up in that competition to date:

<table>
<tr><th></th><th colspan="2">Average of Public Institutions [1]</th><th colspan="2">Average of Private Institutions [1]</th><th>Yale</th></tr>
<tr><th></th><th>1939–40</th><th>1947–48</th><th>1939–40</th><th>1947–48</th><th>1950–51</th></tr>
<tr><td>Per cent of income from:</td><td></td><td></td><td></td><td></td><td></td></tr>
<tr><td>Student fees</td><td>18.6</td><td>31.6 [2]</td><td>52.9</td><td>63.5 [3]</td><td>34</td></tr>
<tr><td>Endowment earnings</td><td>2.3</td><td>1.0</td><td>23.4</td><td>11.8</td><td>37</td></tr>
<tr><td>Gifts and grants</td><td>1.7</td><td>1.9</td><td>12.8</td><td>11.5</td><td>25</td></tr>
<tr><td>Government</td><td>69.2</td><td>56.4</td><td>3.7</td><td>4.4</td><td rowspan="2">4</td></tr>
<tr><td>Other</td><td>8.2</td><td>9.1</td><td>7.2</td><td>8.8</td></tr>
</table>

1. "The Impact of Inflation upon Higher Education," an Interim Statement by the Commission on Financing Higher Education.

2. The 1950 figure was 29.8. *Financing Higher Education in the United States* by John D. Millett (Columbia University Press, 1952), p. 301.

3. The 1950 figure was 67.8. *Ibid.*, p. 300.

We have held our position primarily through the gifts for endowment and for current expenses, of our friends and alumni. Valuable as our student fees are to us, we are generous with scholarships and do not depend on the former as much as we do upon our endowment and gifts. In fact, as I think very few of us realize, we derive almost exactly the same proportion of our income from student fees as do the state universities: 34 per cent in our case, 32 per cent in theirs. We are substantially below the average for private institutions, which is 63.5 per cent. Nor have we increased our student charges as much as other private or even public institutions. The average increase for private universities during the past ten years was 51 per cent; for private liberal arts colleges, 61 per cent; and for state universities' out-of-state fees, 80 per cent. We have raised our undergraduate tuition only 33 per cent. While I think some further increase on our part is indicated, there is a limit beyond which we cannot go lest we restrict our educational benefits to too narrow a circle to do justice to the obligations and opportunities implicit in our mission of leadership.

This limit, together with the practical limit of any substantial exploitation of public sources of income, throws us all the more heavily on our endowment and gifts. Let us see how we have fared in cultivating and replenishing this primary source. As already noted, our income-earning endowment has grown over the past fifty years from 4.9 to 134 million dollars. Simultaneously the Alumni Fund has grown in importance up to its remarkable performances of the past two years, the latter of which produced $1,010,324, a record for all universities in the United States and, for that matter, the world. But the steady inflation of living and maintenance costs has affected us as it has all individuals with fixed incomes, and has pressed us urgently to accumulate new capital. How have we fared in that?

The following figures, taken from a study of gifts and bequests to fifty-one private colleges and universities over the past thirty years, supply the answer:

	Millions of Dollars	Per Cent of Total
1. Over the 30 years Yale ranks second in money received		
a. Harvard	$230	16.3
b. Yale	214	15.1
c. Chicago	121	8.6
d. Northwestern	94	6.7
e. Columbia	76	5.4
2. Between 1920 and 1930 Yale led all 51		
a. Yale	$91	18.6
b. Harvard	83	17.7
c. Chicago	45	9.3
d. Columbia	32	6.6
e. Johns Hopkins	30	6.2
3. Between 1930 and 1940 Yale led all 51		
a. Yale	$77	20.7
b. Harvard	63	16.9
c. Chicago	47	12.7
d. Columbia	22	6.0
e. Northwestern	21	5.6
4. Between 1940 and 1950 Yale fell to second place		
a. Harvard	$84	15.2
b. Yale	46	8.3
c. Northwestern	44	8.0
d. Cornell	35	6.4
e. Princeton	32	5.8

There are two significant facts about these figures. The first is their shrunken purchasing power. The grand total of $112,790,000 reported by all fifty-one institutions for 1949–50 was worth only about $66,000,000 in terms of 1939 dollars. The second fact is that during the past ten years we slipped far behind in the procession we had led for the first twenty. The two facts are not unrelated in present significance. Because our capital accumulation has not kept pace with the inflation of living and operating costs for more than a decade, and because this inflationary trend has been intensified by the Korean war, we are under all the greater pressure to take up the slack.

After a year in which we received more than $10,000,000 (5.9 for endowment, 3.1 for current expenses, and 1.0 from the Alumni Fund) it might be said that we had made a promising start. But it is no more than a start. Nor can we measure it against the goal of $80,000,000 we tentatively set ourselves two years ago. That goal has already been dwarfed by inflation and obscured by the trend of events. Not all these gifts, generous and encouraging as they have been, have sufficed to meet our needs.

I doubt if many people realize the extent to which Yale and her sister universities have suffered from inflation. I have before me a report of the Commission on Financing Higher Education * which calls inflation "the greatest financial peril confronting higher education in the United States today" and warns that our colleges and universities are facing "crippling deficits" or "drastic curtailment of services indispensable to the public interest." This warning was sounded in April 1951. Since then the cost of living has continued to climb until it now stands 86 per cent above 1940.

This has left faculty salaries far behind—so far that, in spite of salary increases of 40 to 50 per cent through the nation at large, college teachers have suffered a net re-

* An independent group of educators, lawyers, and businessmen sponsored by the Association of American Universities (of which Yale is a member) and financed by grants from the Rockefeller Foundation and the Carnegie Corporation.

duction in living standards since 1940 of about 25 per cent. Industrial wages meanwhile have more than kept pace with the cost of living. Between 1940 and 1951 the hourly earnings of workers in manufacturing increased by 138 per cent. At Yale, as elsewhere, the wages of our operating and maintenance staffs have left our teachers' salaries in the lurch. Between 1940 and 1951 the wage scales for operating and maintenance employees at Yale doubled, while the average salary of faculty members rose only about one-third, as follows:

	Percentage Increase 1940 to 1951
Cost of living index	86
Hourly wages of all manufacturing workers, U.S.	138
Faculty salaries, all institutions	40–50
Hourly wages, Yale operating and maintenance employees	100–110
Faculty salaries, Yale	32

Incomes of college teachers have also fallen behind those of other professional people. Between 1940 and 1948 the average dollar income of doctors and dentists more than doubled, while that of lawyers rose by 85 per cent. In 1948, to quote from the commission's statement, "the average income of doctors was about two and one-half times and that of lawyers about two times the average income of college teachers."

Government and industry vie with these professions in outbidding the universities for the services of young men and women with professional training. Government positions now offer considerably more, and industrial positions very much more, than the universities are offering to men of comparable training and ability. Until we put this situation to rights we fail to do justice to our faculty. We run the risk of losing it piecemeal to other occupations, and—a fact we are prone to overlook—we fall ever farther behind in the competition for able recruits to the teaching profession. In other words, we suffer the serious impairment of the most vital of all our resources: the men and women whose inspired teaching and scholarship quickens the whole process of higher education into life. These things are true in general of all our universities. They are particularly and urgently true of one that seeks to maintain a position of leadership.

In the category of plant operation and maintenance, to which we have given much thought at Yale this year, the gap between expenditures and income is even greater than in the educational category. Wage increases combined with shorter work weeks have jacked up labor costs already high before the War. From 1939 to 1948 fuel and lighting costs rose 85 per cent, building materials 120 per cent. And in the border zone between these categories—the libraries, laboratories, museums, galleries, and hospital facilities essential to both teaching and research—operating and maintenance costs often exceeded those of dormitories, dining halls, and classrooms.

We are trying to effect all possible economies in these areas that will not impair the primary educational functions to which no less than 77 per cent of our budget is committed. Shortly before I was appointed, the Corporation engaged outside professional assistance in surveying our administrative and operating costs, which make up respectively the remaining 5 and 18 per cent of our budget. To review the large body of data thus assembled I appointed a Committee on University Organization. This committee has held weekly meetings throughout the year and in addition spent long hours both in study and in consultation with the various University officers in whose fields economies were projected.

The committee has done the University a vital service. Against the normal opposition to change and retrenchment that exists in any institution, and in the face of many logical and economic dilemmas, it has accomplished three things. It has stimulated a healthy revaluation of our noneducational activities in terms of our educational. It is a sign to our alumni and friends that we are not asking for new capital for impractical, luxurious, or wasteful purposes. And it has shown the way to actual economies of some $200,000 in our operating costs, the equivalent of $5,000,000 of new capital.

But while money saved is often as good as money raised, saving itself has its limits of which the *reductio ad absurdum* is 100 per cent. In an institution like Yale growth is to a certain extent a coefficient of health. Quality, not bigness, is our aim. We do not wish to expand in numbers of students or in any purely quantitative way. But quality in both teaching and research means constant improvement of the means to those ends, and this imposes a steady long-run increase in costs.

Our physics laboratory, of which the alumni have heard much this year, is a good illustration of this principle. I shall not repeat here all the reasons why we need this laboratory. I shall simply say that if we wish to keep Yale physics up to our qualitative standards we must have it. If we do not keep Yale physics up to those standards, we neglect not only this basic science itself but all the other sciences, and even the humanities, with which physics, via philosophy, is becoming ever more closely allied. The addition to plant thus becomes an essential *qualitative* need, such as would be normal in any business, and the savings effected by the Committee on University Organization are eclipsed in prospect. Both are healthy, indeed essential. The point is that savings, in the long run, are no substitute for new capital.

Neither are foundation grants. Valuable as these are to us and much as we should like to increase our share of them, they are severely limited, both quantitatively and qualitatively. I am not speaking now of the numerous small private foundations created of late. For our purposes these are identical with the individuals who support them and should therefore be considered in the category of individual gifts. I am speaking of the large philanthropic foundations in which, as in corporations, management is very largely separated from ownership, and policies are determined by directors and trustees. The total contribution of these foundations to American higher education cannot be estimated exactly, but is probably no larger than 2 per cent. Were Yale to double her present income from this source it would still supply less than 3 per cent of her total income. These large foundations support many institutions and enterprises other than educational ones, and in the educational field their operations extend, quite properly, into the public as well as the private institutions. All of which means that, in a purely quantitative sense, they are no substitute for new capital.

Qualitatively their value is limited in several ways. In the first place, their support is not available for such primary needs as the correction of our faculty salary scale or even for such an essential renewal of plant as the new physics laboratory. They are precluded from these both by the small size of their resources in relation to the demands to which they are exposed and by their policy of supporting only pilot studies and programs where they will do the most general good. Invariably these take the form of new projects within the university whose costs the university must eventually assume. In the long run, therefore, foundation grants increase our overhead rather than our financial resources. In a purely material sense they are pump primers, helpful while they last, but helpful in the end only if the pump catches and continues to draw. New projects are all very well, even essential, provided they stay within the proper competence of universities and further the true principles and purposes of higher learning. But they run the danger of accumulating into a series of side shows playing to capacity around an empty main tent. They will not raise our faculty salaries, or build our physics laboratory, or sustain the fundamental curriculum of liberal arts and sciences that is our first responsibility.

As for the government (to consider one more possible source), several obvious things may be said and several not so obvious. In the first place our status as a private university and the principles surrounding it prevent us from seeking more than minimal assistance from this quarter. Although while the G.I. Bill was in effect our share of it was greater, at the moment it amounts to less than 2 per cent of our total income—for the most part in contracts for medical and strategic scientific research. It is possible, of course, that this type of work may expand; that a new G.I. Bill for veterans of the Korean war may be enacted; or that general federal subsidies in support of medical education may be forthcoming. Allowing for all these possibilities it stands to reason that we cannot expect much help from public sources already committed, both in principle and in fact, to public education.

What we can and should expect is a considered public

policy that will enable us to continue on our own resources. The recent report of President Truman's Commission on Higher Education contemplates the maintenance of a vigorous system of private education as a matter of principle and a desirable goal of public policy. To provide for its needs the commission recommended both federal and state tax remissions conducive to gifts and bequests to private institutions and respectful of their present areas of tax immunity. But while these remissions have to some extent encouraged the flow of private funds into higher education, continued, uncontrolled inflation reduces their net value; and what is worse, they are accompanied by both federal and state efforts to whittle down our tax immunities that cancel their benefits at the source. The Treasury Department's policy of maintaining low interest rates is resulting in progressively lower yields from endowment. The rising level of personal income taxes makes giving ever more difficult, especially for those in the middle-income brackets on whom we rely so heavily for support. On balance, the fiscal operations of government are strongly, though no doubt unintentionally, adverse to private education. They do not provide the positive support recommended by the President's commission and urgently needed by the private institutions if they are in fact to survive.

No matter where we start, every spoke of the wheel leads to the hub: the need for new capital. I have cited faculty salaries and the physics laboratory as cases in point. Let me select another illustration from the scores of reports submitted to me at the end of the year. The masters of our colleges all complain about overcrowding and argue with cogency that if the original purpose of the colleges as something more than mere dormitories is to be salvaged their enrollment should be reduced. Let us assume, for the moment, that the masters would be satisfied with the average reduction of fifty students per college suggested by some of them. This would mean a total reduction in enrollment of five hundred, or a possible reduction in tuition and room rent of as much as $462,500. This loss of general income would have serious consequences, not only for the colleges themselves but for many other activities with which the masters, as members of the faculty, are vitally concerned. The result: a continuing dilemma that could be duplicated in one form or another in practically all our schools and departments of instruction, none of which can be satisfactorily resolved save by the infusion of new funds.

With all the savings we have accomplished and gifts we have received to date, we are barely keeping abreast of things and are making slight progress toward our proper goals. It is true that, in the first year of the Korean war, our worst fears did not materialize. The total war that so many of us expected did not—in that year—occur. With the improvement of the United Nations' position and the adoption of the present military service policy, the anticipated decrease in enrollment of 40 per cent shrank to a mere 1 per cent, so that we enter the present academic year with a student body about the same size as last year's.* A reduction of 40 per cent would have meant a loss in tuition and room rent of something like $2,500,000. We can say that we are ahead of the game; but this would be merely saying, like the Red Queen in *Through the Looking Glass,* that we are running hard to keep in the same place.

We need new capital, above all the unrestricted capital

* See the table on page 62.

ENROLLMENT:

	Candidates for degrees or certificates	Others not candidates for degrees or certificates	Candidates for degrees or certificates	Others not candidates for degrees or certificates
Freshman Year	1,168			
Yale College	2,446	3		
School of Engineering, Undergraduate Division	583			
Total undergraduate schools			4,197	3
Graduate School (including Sheffield Scientific School)	1,089	154		
School of Engineering, Graduate Division	99			
School of Medicine	308	103		
Divinity School	402			
Law School	551	21		
School of the Fine Arts	350	17		
School of Music	125	3		
School of Forestry	28			
School of Nursing	121			
Bureau of Highway Traffic		23		
Institute of Far Eastern Languages		93		
Research fellows		60		
Total enrollment, graduate and professional schools			3,073	474
			7,270	477
Deduct for duplicate registrations			59	
Total candidates for degrees or certificates			7,211	
Others not candidates for degrees or certificates			477	
Total individual enrollment			7,688	

normally required by any business for policy-making scope and administrative discretion. If this capital is not to be found in its customary form, we must find it in new forms that will serve the same purpose. If, for example, corporations are effectively to supplement individual philanthropy in American higher education, we must encourage them to move far beyond the narrow *quid pro quo* basis to which they are at present moored by obligations to their stockholders and, as Alfred Sloan has sensibly argued, to extend their support to the basic liberal arts and sciences as well as to the applied sciences and technology. To propose the specific ways and means of obtaining the resources we need is beyond the scope of this report. My purpose was to state the problem, and I shall be content if I have succeeded in that. Its solution is the most urgent item of business on Yale's agenda.

We are all responsible for that agenda—students, faculty, and alumni. Difficult as it is, I believe that once we all face that responsibility we shall be capable of discharging it. I base this conviction on two fundamental considerations. The first is that there is enough wealth in the United States to provide for the needs of all our colleges and universities, indeed for our entire educational system, and provide for them liberally, if the will accompanies the resources. If we doubled our present national expenditures on higher education they would barely equal 1 per cent of our total gross product. The problem is to inculcate the will, not to create the resources. The second consideration is that among our own friends and alumni there is a higher proportion of both the will and the resources than there is in the nation. This is proved, I think, by the record-breaking performances of the Alumni Fund during the past two years, as well as by the capital gifts we have received.

We have earned this much encouragement, have we not, because we have been able, in spite of everything, to hold up to public scrutiny a record and a purpose of vital consequence to our civilization. This civilization is now beset by powerful enemies who would destroy it. They outnumber us. They are unremitting in their efforts to foment local wars they hope will exhaust us. They are willing to gamble on global war. Their pressure puts every basic institution in our society under strain, not only for weapons for defense but for the wisdom for defense. There is, I submit, no such contradiction between the needs of higher education and the needs of national defense as has sometimes been taken for granted in the debate on the subject. On the contrary, I think there never was a time when higher education had so much to offer in a national emergency. Our faculty does not need to be convinced of this. Once the alumni see it and our students, who will soon join their ranks, show by their conduct that they see it too, we shall all then see a long way into the future and, I am confident, discover the resources we need to realize our hopes for it.

National Book Awards Address

(Speech to the literary profession gathered for the third annual Awards, New York, January 29, 1952)

If ever coals were brought to Newcastle I bring them today. What can I say to the writers, publishers, booksellers, printers, and critics of books whose collected works are called the true universities? I am more than humble. I am desperate. I read my fate in the diary of James Hadley, Professor of Greek in Yale College from 1854 to 1872 and father of President Hadley. Returning from a faculty meeting in the year 1852, he foretells my present circumstances as follows:

> The state of things at Western Reserve College is really deplorable, and the case of Mr. Pierce, their President, is in some respects a hard one. They have kept him begging for 6 years or more, and now complain that he is fit for nothing else. Mr. Olmsted having said something about the attempts of alumni in Amherst and Williams to dictate in regard to

> College matters, Mr. Woolsey said, "Mark my prediction: if our alumni meet together year after year, with nothing to do but talk, and time enough for that, they will be trying to govern us. You must shut their mouths with long addresses."

My case, too, is a hard one. Begging and—shall we say medium length—addresses and the intricacies of what my friend President Conant calls "academical superintendence" have removed me from your company which I once greatly cherished, removed me so far that I am safe even from guilt by association, busted me back through the ranks from writer to reader, all the way back to general reader, private first class. Gone are the orgies of reading that began, for me, with *Leatherstocking Tales* and *Froissart's Chronicle,* that continued, albeit, under competition, through school and college, and that became standard fare in graduate school and teaching days. All I have been able to salvage is the habit of reading myself to sleep every night. I have kept this same habit (and by skillful use of spotlights and sleepshades, the same wife) for nearly twenty-five years. In, on, and under our bedside table is a motley library for every mood. It includes at the moment, Shakespeare, Shaw, Plutarch, Joseph Swain's *Ancient World,* Francis Biddle's *Fear of Freedom,* United States Reports Vol. 341 (containing the Supreme Court's opinions affirming the conviction of the Communist party officials), Roland H. Bainton's *Travail of Religious Liberty,* Elliot Paul's *Black Gardenia,* A. P. Herbert's *Number Nine or the Mind Sweepers;* Volumes 2 and 3 of the Princeton University Press edition of *The Papers of Thomas Jefferson;* the Treasurer's Report of Yale University (in case of late calls from alumni), and the New Testament. It is a wonderful pharmacopoeia, more potent than sleeping pills when I wish to sleep or coffee when I wish to stay awake. It is the consolation of my academical superintendence. It is all I have to justify my claim to address you this afternoon as anything but a technological illiterate.

My narrow escape from technological illiteracy—if indeed it prove to be an escape and not just temporary immunity—causes me to ponder the fate of our country, in which this disease is endemic and is spreading like the elm blight. What happens when we are all too busy to read, when our ways of life and work combined with the substitutes for reading now in mass production and use finally conquer our taste for reading as well as our belief in its utility? I know—my own metaphor implies it—that you can drug yourself with reading. I know that there are "sermons in stones and books in the running brooks." As a teacher of young men for nearly a quarter century, I have been unusually sensitive to their elders' appeals to experience and action. Ours is an age of action, hair-trigger action, and we cannot resign from it. But what is to become of us when action no longer finds inspiration or discipline in thought because thought has not been able to find inspiration or discipline in books?

Is the question rhetorical? I do not think so. There was a day in the history of this republic when its men of affairs found time to read and demonstrated, in their own lives and works, the utility as well as the delight of reading. The four master builders, Hamilton, John Adams, Jefferson, and Madison, were probably the four most widely read men of their age. Certainly this was true of Adams, Jefferson, and Madison, and it might have been true of the impetuous Hamilton had he survived his impetuosity. For we find him at eighteen as an undergraduate student as deep in the classics of law and philosophy as his more studious collaborator on *The Federalist* of a decade later.

Our prize-winning poet, Miss Moore, says of poetic images, "these things are important not because . . . a high-sounding interpretation can be put upon them but because they are useful." Never, to my knowledge, did men find more practical and more immediate use in reading than these four. Between them, though they were in politics all their lives, in an age of intermittent war and revolution, serving as congressional delegates, ambassadors, governors, constitution makers, cabinet members and presidents, they read virtually every book in print in the western world. And out of all this reading? It had very little application to any particular views, says Adams somewhat disingenuously of his own case,

> till these debates in Congress and the interrogatories in public and private, turned my thoughts to these researches, which produced the *Thoughts on Government,* the Constitution of Massachusetts, and at length the *Defence of the Constitutions of the United States,* and the *Discourses on Davila,* writings which have never done any good to me, though some of them undoubtedly contributed to produce the Constitution of New York, the Constitution of the U.S., and the last Constitutions of Pennsylvania and Georgia. They undoubtedly, also, contributed to the writings of Publius, called the Federalist, which were all written after the publication of my work in Philadelphia, New York, and Boston.

The reading lists of Jefferson and Madison and the historical accomplishments of the four men establish beyond cavil the general validity of Adam's claim. Do you know these lists? Let me cite Jefferson's education for a lawyer. "Till eight o'clock in the morning"—not from eight but till eight—he prescribes the reading of books on Physical Studies, Ethics, Religion and Natural Law; from eight to twelve, Law; from twelve to one, Politics and Political Economy; in the afternoon, History; and "From Dark to Bedtime," Belles Lettres, Criticism, Rhetoric and Oratory. Each subject is subdivided categorically and ballasted by scores of titles, all of which Jefferson had read himself. His Literary Bible and Commonplace Book expand this list, as do his letters, particularly those to his nephew Peter Carr, until, as I have said, it includes virtually every book in print in the western world.

This was no bibliolatry. It was the earnest, inner, creative life of a man who taught himself at least three ancient and four modern foreign languages so that he might pursue the uses of reading to their ultimate limits. Out of this life, which he shared most intimately with Adams and Madison, came the charters of American democracy: the Declaration of Independence, the state constitutions with their bills of rights; the Federal Constitution with its Bill of Rights; the Bill for the More General Diffusion of Knowledge and the Bill for Establishing Religious Freedom in Virginia; the public documents and state papers embedded in a matrix of private correspondence which the three men kept up to within a few days of their deaths (and they all outlived the biblical span), Jefferson in a hand painfully crippled by a broken wrist, Adams till his hand and wrist became so weak from old age that he had to dictate to his niece; a body of writing which in Jefferson's case, in the definitive edition now in preparation at Princeton, is expected to fill over fifty volumes, and to which again in Jefferson's case, Abraham Lincoln, another great reader, said he turned whenever he wished to refer to the "definitions and axioms of free society."

So much for the uses of reading in that age. What of our own age, in which war and revolution are putting those definitions and axioms to the severest test they have endured since birth? In Washington, I learn, a university is about to open a course for ghost writers, who "will be taught to write in such a way that orators will understand at all times what they are saying." Ghost writers are "indispensable artisans," an official of the university declares. There are "more than 150 of them on the top level in Washington alone. Most of the great speeches we hear are written in whole or in part by someone backstage." The writers of these speeches have a hard time adjusting their talents "to fit the mental and oratorical capacities" of the men for whom they are writing. Hence the course. What advice and counsel could these indispensable artisans obtain from Jefferson? Suppose, by chance, they turned to his letter to Peter Carr in 1785, when Jefferson was ambassador to France and his nephew was just entering upon his serious studies:

> It is time for you now to begin to be choice in your reading . . . I advise you to begin a course of ancient history, reading everything in the original and not in translation. First read Goldsmith's history of Greece. This will give you a digested view of that field. Then take up ancient history in the detail, reading the following books, in the following or-

der: Herodotus, Thucydides, Xenophontis Anabasis, Arrian, Quintus Curtius, Diodorus Siculus, Justin. This shall form the first stage of your historical reading, and is all I need mention to you now. The next will be of Roman history (Livy, Sallust, Caesar, Cicero's epistles, Suetonius, Tacitus, Gibbon). In Greek and Latin poetry you . . . will read . . . Virgil, Terence, Horace, Anacreon, Theocritus, Homer, Euripides, Sophocles. Read also Milton . . . , Shakespeare, Ossian, Pope's and Swift's works, in order to form your style in your own language. In morality, read Epictetus, Xenophontis Memorabilia, Plato's Socratic dialogues, Cicero's philosophies, Antoninus and Seneca.

What would our ghost writers say to this? The very reading of the words puts a hex on their profession.

"Reading," in Bacon's aphorism, "maketh a full man, conference a ready man, and writing an exact man." What are we doing under our forest of television masts, with our indispensable artisans the ghost writers, our analysts, opinion samplers, and committees of brainpickers? We are succumbing one by one to technological illiteracy. We have traded in the mind's eye for the eye's mind. We are conferring. We have not quite given up reading. Here and there, in a few homes, in a few educational institutions, it still hangs on in competition with more efficient methods and processes, such as the extrasensory and the audiovisual. A few teachers still prefer written essays to intellectual bingo games that can be scored by electricity. A few students still like to read, a few statesmen, I suppose, still carry books with them when they travel. I am still reading in bed, and you ladies and gentlemen of the book world are still earning a modest competence.

But what if present trends continue? Since reading maketh us full men, when we stop reading we shall be empty men. Since men who do not read have no use for writing, and in any case empty men have nothing to write about, we shall stop writing. We shall then be empty and inexact, though presumably we shall still be able to confer and conference will still make us ready. Ready for what? For some technological *deus ex machina* to finish the plot we have forgotten how to write? For some graduate of the school for ghost writers to whisper to us from the prompter's box?

They will not serve us. They cannot promote the more general diffusion of knowledge essential to a democratic society because they are mere transmitters; they cannot inform the statesmen to whom that society must look for the preservation and renewal of its charters because they are themselves uninformed. During the past century the average working week of our industrial and white collar workers has shrunk from seventy to less than forty hours. The millions of man hours thus conserved form the new Colossus. This Colossus has more leisure at his disposal than all the aristocracies of history, all the patrons of art, all the captains of industry and kings of enterprise. What will he do with it? Will he read? Will he make himself a full man and an exact man, or will he be content to be merely a ready man—a measure of muscle and a shout from the mob? The choice lies before him. Who will help him make it?

Ladies and gentlemen of the world of books, as an academical superintendent I make common cause with you. I hope *we* will!

Alumni Day Address

(Speech to the annual gathering of Yale graduates, New Haven, February 22, 1952)

Since I assumed my present office, not yet two years ago, I have been at pains to alert all members of the Yale community—students, faculty and alumni—to the extraordinary dangers that stand in our path. It would be more appropriate to this festival year to celebrate the solid accomplishments and the going concerns that make Yale what she undoubtedly is, one of the greatest universities in the modern world. But this world is too much with us for celebration. Yale still faces three major tests set for her by circumstances beyond her control, all three of which she must pass before her future as a private institution of higher learning will be secure. The first and most obvious of these is the test of war. The second is a test compounded of economic factors, the worst of which are inflation and an indifferent public policy that gives lip service to the survival of the private universities but makes inadequate provision for its accomplishment. The third is a cultural test, a proof of our ability as a people to understand the fundamental aims and principles of a university and, having understood them, of our willingness to give them support.

When I addressed you on this occasion last year the Korean war seemed likely at any moment to explode into the third and perhaps final world war. Military service and educational policies were under discussion which might have reduced our student body by as much as 40 per cent (and our income in proportion) and forced upon us a ruinous system of curricular acceleration. Worse still, from every point of view, was the way in which this discussion tended to oppose the interests of higher education to the national interest, as two distinct and antithetical considerations.

A year has gone by, and although the Korean war continues to exact its bitter toll and the Kremlin continues to blow other coals through its long tubes, I think we may discern some improvement in our fortunes in this ironically named cold war. We have held our ground in Korea. We have converted our economy to the needs of war without suffering the collapse so hopefully predicted by the Communists. And, despite the slow development of grander designs, we have, with our allies in the North Atlantic Treaty Organization, made solid progress in the defense of western Europe. I make these observations not as an expert analysis of world affairs but to emphasize the fact—and I should like to give it all possible emphasis—that the fortunes of Yale like the fortunes of our country still ride the fortunes of war.

A year ago I referred to these circumstances as a crisis. Today I should refer to them as a condition. The word "crisis" has lost its meaning in hyperbole. This is the nature of our age, and we must learn to live with it. Are we learning? I see some signs in the affirmative. The military service and educational policies at present under discussion in Washington and elsewhere throughout the nation, and the tone and quality of the discussion itself, show less of a tendency to scrap higher education as an expendable in an imaginary short-run emergency and more of a tendency to integrate it as an essential with our long-run cultural, political, and military needs. These are encouraging signs. They are signs of intellectual maturity, of a national realization of the utility of learning even in its least utilitarian aspects.

All this is to the good, but it leaves much unfinished business on our hands. We at Yale have more than our share of this business. There is the old story of the American visitor to Cambridge University who, marveling at the lush parklike lawns known as "The Backs" and asking an ancient gardener their secret, was told, "Oh, you mow 'em and you roll 'em and you roll 'em and you mow 'em for six hundred years." The same long, patient effort underlies the educational standards of Cambridge and her lineal descendants, Harvard, Yale, and Princeton. To make these standards the rule rather than the exception in the United States may not take six hundred years, but it will take a good many, and much devotion and not a little heartbreak; and if Yale is to play the part in the process to which her tradition and ideals and, as I have argued elsewhere, her very economic interests commit her, she must constantly strive to keep ahead of the standards as the leveling progresses.

I have dwelt so constantly on the second test, the economic, during the past two years, that I am beginning to feel like an economist—in Thomas Carlyle's sense of the term, who called economics "the dismal science." In the files of Woodbridge Hall the other day, I came upon the following comment by President Dwight in 1897. Referring to the temporarily satisfactory condition of the University budget, he said: "This condition of things cannot, however, continue for any considerable period of years, owing to the marked decrease in the rate of interest, which is already noticeable. Such a fall indicates, of course, a serious diminution of income to the University for which there is only one possible remedy, namely a large increase in endowments."

This statement of the case is as accurate today, when in terms of our educational standards and the financial resources available to private institutions we must compete at odds of something like seventeen to one against us, as it was in 1897 when we faced no such competitive disadvantage. I have shown in my recent annual report how these odds are computed, and I have concluded from them, in unwitting paraphrase of President Dwight, "No matter where we start, every spoke of the wheel leads to the hub: the need for new capital." Of this economic test, severe as it is, I should say with the same cautious optimism what I said of the test of war. I believe we are passing it—at all events, I believe we can pass it.

The cultural test, which must cap the climax, is more difficult; and it is to this that I should like to direct particular attention this afternoon. For all our efforts to integrate higher education with our long-run needs and to solve its financial problems will have been in vain if we fail to understand the true nature and purposes of our universities.

These purposes are to carry on the quest for the ultimate truths concerning man and his place in the universe that began with the ancient Greeks and Hebrews—man's age-old effort to rise above his passions and put his powers of reason and conscience to the service of his fellow men —and to prepare our students not just for intellectual or vocational pursuits but for the whole of life as free men in a free society. This is the responsibility Yale shares with her sister universities. This is the mission of higher education in a troubled world.

But if this is their responsibility and their mission, it is also true that the very society that asks and expects so much of them has periodically attacked the universities. Oxford stands on bloody grounds. Cambridge owes its origin to a migration from Oxford following a riot. Oxford traces a similar lineage to Paris. French and Italian universities have had their share of strife with both church and state. In the nineteenth century the Germans exalted their universities and in the twentieth they debased them. Only in Great Britain, France (save during the Occupation), and the United States, among the countries mentioned, do we find relatively long, unbroken periods of calm in the relations between the universities and society; and even now, in the United States, this calm is ruffled.

I leave it to others to analyze this strange ambivalence in our society, which alternately cherishes and despises its institutions of higher learning. In it, I suppose, they may find lingering elements of frontier life as well as much of our national obsession with the utilitarian and the practical. In it, too, are tensions between contemporaries who drift apart into speculative and practical affairs, into what the army calls the ancient war between staff and line; the simple semantic differences that H. T. Webster has so eloquently lampooned as "shop talk"; the eternal difference between the world as the alumnus knew it when he graduated and the world as it is today. All of these tensions and differences, now aggravated by politics and the threat of global war, have afflicted our universities and here and there hampered them in the performance of their duties, though they have not yet greatly shaken their fundamental stability.

There are several reasons for this, all subtly interwoven. The first is that the British universities and their American descendants were, as Yale still is, private foundations; and they bequeathed their tradition to the public institutions founded in their image. If this inheritance has been misused from time to time the results of the misuse have only proved the strength of the tradition. The true university, in the Anglo-American world, cherishes its independence as much as the private citizen, and bases its claim to that independence on the same constitutional rights and privileges.

These rights and privileges constitute a second reason for the stability and independence of British and American universities. The fact is that Great Britain and the United States, the true founders and exemplars of modern democracy, uphold national bills of rights; and although these bills are constantly under attack, as their authors knew and predicted they would be, they show a stubborn capacity for survival. Article I of the Constitution of the United States guaranteeing the writ of habeas corpus and prohibiting bills of attainder and *ex post facto* laws; the First Amendment, which reads, "Congress shall make no law respecting an establishment of religion, or prohibiting the free exercise thereof; or abridging the freedom of speech, or of the press; or the right of the people peaceably to assemble, and to petition the government for a redress of grievances"; the Fifth Amendment, guaranteeing due process of law; the Sixth Amendment, guaranteeing jury trial and the right of the accused to counsel—most of us tend to take these articles and amendments for granted. Yet centuries of human suffering, human compassion, and human wisdom speak out in their familiar phrases. In the conscience of our people they possess the strength of armies. They communicate this strength to our free press, our free churches, our free political institutions—and our free universities.

A third reason for the stability and independence of our universities is the practical value of freedom. We are fond of saying that it was free enterprise that made this country great. I would say the same of its universities. Not only did free enterprise produce the wealth that provided their material resources. Free enterprise for their faculties enabled those faculties to provide equally strong intellectual and spiritual resources to the generations of students that passed through their classrooms. The solid contributions of these college graduates to the welfare of our country are evident in its historical records. In these Yale has shared, and is now sharing, with distinction.

This educational philosophy, this free enterprise in ideas, rests on the conviction that freedom is a source of strength, not of weakness. It holds that the only true loyalty is the loyalty of men who give it voluntarily, not under compulsion; that the only true religious faith is one that can withstand knowledge of the world in the fullness thereof, as Christ Himself withstood it with Satan on the mountaintop; that the only true learning is the learning of the scholar who is free to pursue his explorations whither he will. Out of this educational philosophy, and the democratic political philosophy of which it is a part, have come achievements of the human mind and the human spirit in every sphere of life and thought that have imparted great strength to our society—great books, great scientific discoveries, great, luminous ideas of social justice and political enlightenment, unparalleled industrial accomplishments, great military victories, enduring visions of world peace, and above all, great men and women, men and women of conscience and character who have demonstrated in their good works, their humility, and their essential respect for the dignity of man the highest ideals of our educational system.

Are there any reasons, then, for renouncing an educational philosophy that has served us so well for so long a time?

The Communists, of course, would like us to, for they represent an educational philosophy that is the absolute negation of ours. I do not intend to lecture you on the methods by which science, art, history, philology, music, literary criticism, economics, and philosophy are prefabricated in the Kremlin. I am not privy to those occult secrets, black arts as they would have been called in days gone by, red arts as they must be called today. Nor do I have to tell you how the Communists run their universities. They are a hideous example of what can happen when the freedom of the individual is totally destroyed and the enslavement of his mind becomes complete. The example is so hideous, so repugnant to our educational traditions and so abhorrent to the faculties of Yale and her sister universities, that I do not think we need dwell too long on the Kremlin's curriculum as an alternative to our own. As a teacher in Yale College and the Graduate School for twenty years, I know what it is like to be heckled by students and contradicted by colleagues, but I cannot even imagine what it is like to be spied upon and censored. How any creative or honest mind can be attracted to or supported by such methods is beyond my comprehension. As an armchair strategist, I find the Soviet educational system a strategic asset to the United States.

But what of our own people who would combat the menace of communism by limiting the freedom of our universities and prescribing through outside political or other nonprofessional authority what they shall teach? This, too, would mean a renunciation of our educational philosophy, or some of it, if it is possible to renounce some without renouncing all. If the people who make these recommendations assume or suspect that our universities are deliberately abetting the menace of communism, I would respectfully say that they are mistaken. If they base their proposals on the theory that such a censored and supervised curriculum would produce sounder teaching, I would give them John Milton's answer from his *Areopagitica:*

> How can a man teach with authority, which is the life of teaching, how can he be a doctor in his book as he ought to be, or else had better be silent, whenas all he teaches, all he delivers, is but under the tuition, under the correction of his patriarchal licenser to blot or alter what precisely accords not with the hide-bound humor which he calls his judgment?

If they contemplate the sounder training of students, men who can be counted on to fight the good fight in the cause of freedom, I give them John Stuart Mill's essay, "Of Thought and Discussion," in which he says,

> The greatest orator, save one, of antiquity, has left it on record that he always studied his adversary's case with as great, if not greater, intensity than even his own. What Cicero practiced as the means of forensic success requires to be imitated by all who study any subject in order to arrive at the truth. He who knows only his own side of the case knows little of that. His reasons may be good, and no one may be able to refute them. But if he is equally unable to refute the reasons on the opposite side; if he does not so much as know what they are, he has no ground for preferring either opinion.

Would it be a sound preparation for life in a free society to deny both students and teachers, as such, rights they enjoy as citizens? Would this not constitute a vote of no confidence, not only in the men themselves but in the society for which they were preparing? And is confidence to be won by votes of no confidence? There is, I repeat, a practical value in freedom. John Milton and John Stuart Mill were no relativists. They were strict judges of right and wrong, uncompromising individualists and believers in free enterprise. There is an impressive weight of evidence on their side, of which the greatest of all is the Bible. "Good and evil we know in the field of this world grow up together almost inseparably," says Milton. "He that can apprehend and consider vice with all her baits and seeming pleasures, and yet abstain, and yet distinguish, and yet prefer that which is truly better, he is the true warfaring Christian." And by the same token, I would add, he and only he is the true defender of democracy.

I conclude then that our traditional educational policy

is the true safeguard against the menace of communism and that therefore we should not renounce it, in whole or in part; and on behalf of the Corporation and Faculty of Yale University, I declare that we have no intention of so doing. On the contrary, we intend to maintain and strengthen this policy.

I have had a good deal of advice during the past twenty months in what is called public relations, particularly in the advanced postgraduate branch of that science known as alumni relations. I am a poor student. Far from mastering the science, I do not even believe that it exists. For my private tutor in the subject is Plutarch, who, rebuking Pericles for arranging his affability and staging his chance appearances in public, declares: "Real excellence, indeed, is most recognized when most openly looked into; and in really good men, nothing which meets the eyes of external observers so truly deserves their admiration, as their daily common life does that of their nearer friends." That is the strength of Yale University. That is what gives me confidence that we shall pass all our tests.

A Little Learning

(The Stearns lecture delivered at
Phillips Academy, Andover, May 2, 1952)

A little learning is a dangerous thing;
Drink deep, or taste not the Pierian spring:
There shallow draughts intoxicate the brain,
And drinking largely sobers us again.

I take my title from these familiar lines of Alexander Pope's *Essay on Criticism.* The Pierian spring was the spring in North Thessaly from which the Muses drank and so refreshed the wisdom and skill in the arts and sciences with which they inspired the human race. It was the symbol of pure learning and revered as such in Greek mythology. It was the *fons et origo* of a culture that exalted truth, beauty, reason, and freedom, that became the foundation of western civilization, and that still inspires the free nations in their effort to preserve that civilization.

We have done away with this mythology and with it, I sometimes think, all but done away with the culture that supported it (and was supported by it) as well. We have made a monkey out of Prometheus with our cyclotrons. We have left Mercury in the lurch with our jets. We have discarded the Muses and their spring for teachers and books, and we are in the process of discarding the teachers and books for television and other mechanical marvels. We might better express Alexander Pope's sentiments as follows:

> A little learning is a difficult thing—
> How *far* is it to the Pierian spring?
> Let's have a quick one at the nearest bar,
> Or better still, curb-service in the car.

Or we might render it:

> A little learning *is* a dangerous thing:
> There may be poison in the Pierian spring!
> They say it's Greek, but when we hear it gushin',
> It sounds to us suspiciously like Russian!

This is a strange state of mind, is it not, for a people who more than three hundred years ago (1647) adopted the first general education act in modern times and founded nine colleges before achieving their independence. It is a strange state of mind for the descendants of Puritans who recognized ignorance as the chief weapon of "that old deluder, Satan," and the heirs of Thomas Jefferson who saw it as the chief instrument of dictators and despots. It is a paradox in a nation that has led the world in bringing educational opportunities to its citizens and today sends more of them to school and college than any other free people has ever done in history.

Have I exaggerated our national attitude toward education? You can cite individual cases to prove that I have. This school is one. My university, I like to think, is another. But the attitude I describe is far too prevalent for those who have the welfare of American education at heart to be complacent about it, and even at Andover and Yale the attitude is not unknown. As a nation and a civilization we have wandered far from the Pierian spring, into an arid land where the waters of that spring are blended, bottled, and purveyed under a variety of persuasive labels but where, of the spring's pure essence, it is a long time between drinks. Here, intoxicated by blends and substitutes, we dispute the merits of the original without really tasting it, after the fashion of tipplers, confused yet sure of ourselves, to the detriment of our educational system and the equal detriment of our civilization and our country.

The pure essence that is so much wanting in our educational system is that which has for its purpose neither the filling of categories with quantitative knowledge nor the communication of vocational skills, but the awakening and development of the intellectual, moral, and aesthetic powers in man. This purpose is admirably stated in the recent report of a committee on general education, in the organization of which your headmaster was a prime mover. A liberal education, says this report, should help to "achieve the excellence of human nature," to instill in the individual such qualities as intellectual curiosity, a love of excellence, inner strength and integrity, and above all, the capacity for self-education. To achieve these results, the committee insists on three indispensable prerequisites: first, the recruiting and encouraging of imaginative, enthusiastic, creative teachers; second, making education a more personal affair through tutorials, seminars, and small courses; third, more active participation and personal involvement in the part of the student in the educational process, in distinction to the passive absorption of materials.

With all due credit to those individual schools and colleges that are making progress toward these goals, and with high hopes that they may sustain their momentum, we must face the fact that the country as a whole has neither adopted the goals nor set aside enough of its resources even to keep within sight of them. Our committee gives top priority to the recruitment of "imaginative, enthusiastic, and creative teachers" and calls for a much higher ratio of teachers of this caliber to students. Yet according to an editorial in the *New York Times* we graduated from college this year only 32,000 teachers of all calibers to meet a nationwide demand for 160,000. This demand, by the way, is calculated not on the basis of small seminars that will make education an individual experience but on the minimum ratio of teachers to students and classrooms that will bring the students in off the fire escapes without increasing the local tax rate. As to the quality of this teaching, you may draw your own conclusions from the facts that of 600,000 elementary teachers in our public schools, 300,000 do not hold college degrees and, according to the National Education Association, 100,000 are so poorly prepared that their continued presence in the classroom is considered "dangerous to the mental and emotional health of America's youth."

There are reasons for these conditions, but there is no excuse. A principal reason is the low salaries paid to teachers, ranging on the average in our public schools from a high of $4,500 in New York to a low of $1,475 in Mississippi, for a national average of $3,290. In 1950 the average annual earnings per full-time employee in

American agriculture and industry were $3,024. The comparable figure for public school teachers that year was $3,097. There is this significant difference between the two figures. The first, the industrial, is an average of skilled and unskilled wages. The second, the educational, is an average of salaries paid to a skilled profession. The fact that the two figures are very nearly equal shows better than words not only the relative position of teaching in our national scale of values but also the teaching profession's relatively feeble powers of competition for the kind of recruits it needs. If we compare our average teacher's salary with the average salary of college graduates in other professions, we find 95 per cent of the latter earning $3,000 or over, 79 per cent earning $5,000 or over, and 59 per cent earning $7,500 or over.

No one expects to get rich in teaching. We all take a vow of poverty when we enter the profession. But if a teacher is to fulfill the requirements set for him by our committee, he must be able to share liberally in the cultural opportunities of his fellow men—raise a family, read, travel, cultivate his intellectual and aesthetic tastes. Alas, he cannot afford these essentials. He has all he can do to pay the grocer.

I know one excellent schoolteacher who spends his summers running a hot-dog stand in an amusement park so that he can afford to stick by his profession the rest of the year. He should be reading Plato. Or better still Aristotle. Or writing a book.

The plain fact is that the teaching profession is cut off from the type of recruits it most urgently needs *at the source,* in our colleges, where hundreds of actual candidates and thousands of potential ones are lost every year to other professions. Money alone will not rectify these conditions. Every teacher must have a sense of mission. But until we pay our teachers a wage that enables them to fulfill that mission our efforts to improve upon it with curricular reforms will be futile and we shall continue to suffer an enormous waste of cultural and human resources.

We do not tolerate such a state of affairs in industry. Why do we tolerate it in education? Our excuse is that we cannot afford to do better. How valid is this excuse? In 1950 the gross national product of the United States —that is, the total market value of all goods and services produced—was $282,000,000,000. Our educational expenditures that year, both public and private, were approximately $5,600,000 on primary and secondary education and $2,200,000 on higher education, a total of $7,800,000 or 2.7 per cent of our gross national product.

I will not compare this expenditure with our defense budget as I do not wish to suggest that the latter should be reduced. But I will compare it with consumer expenditures on radio, television sets, and musical instruments (with the last finishing a very poor third) of $3,120,000,000 or 1.1 per cent of our gross product, and with expenditures on new and used cars, not counting trucks, of $19,447,000,000 or 6.9 per cent of our gross product. These figures and others showing the amounts we spend each year on pleasures and creature comforts quite apart from our necessities prove to my satisfaction, at least, that we could spend more on education: as much more as is needed to accomplish the goals we are discussing. Our excuse that we cannot afford to do so is a lame one. The truth is that we do not wish to do so. This is not because we are obdurate and hard-hearted. It is because we are deluded—deluded by a little learning. That is all we are paying for and all we are getting for our money. It is a cultural, not an economic, phenomenon, though it does have an economic reckoning. For the sums we imagine we are saving on education are spent on juvenile delinquency and other social and economic diseases which education might have cured at half the cost.

Is there no compromise, no substitute for able teachers? Are there no curricular devices that will compensate for the lack of them? Here our delusions multiply, and vocationalism, unrelated gobbets of quantitative knowledge, and downright nature-faking crowd liberal learning to the wall. In our nationwide secondary school curriculum, the milieu in which millions of individuals plan their lives each year, courses in office training, commercial occupation, effective living, band music, and radio broadcasting press heavily on the serried remnants of the liberal arts.

I do not assume that every student in our secondary schools can or should go to college, nor do I question the motive behind such "vocational" courses for those who do not. But I do question the results. For students who go on to college they represent not only a waste of time but a confusion of values that has made serious inroads into higher education. For those who do not go on, they are poor substitutes for vocational apprenticeship and the subjective experience of life itself. There is too great a tendency in the United States, even on the part of individuals who admit the value of a liberal education to students preparing for college and the professions, to discount its value to those for whom secondary school is the final educational experience. Too many of us are disposed to agree with Bentham's view that in the enjoyment of life "pushpin is as good as poetry," and, out of ignorance, laziness, or sometimes out of intellectual snobbery, and on the basis of highly inexact and often haphazard methods of selection, to relegate lives to pushpin that might have been redeemed by poetry.

I shall have more to say on this subject presently. Let me say here that I believe that for *all* students, those who go on to college and those who do not, the richer the experience of liberal education, limited only by the individual's capacity to assimilate it, the better for our culture and the better for our country; and that in relation to this type of education the type I am criticizing bulks far too large.

This is no condescending lament from the ivory tower. It is the plea of students who have been through the mill and who deserve better of their country than it is giving them. Let me cite one of them who might almost be said to have died in this cause. He is Bert Stiles, author of the recently published war book, *Serenade to the Big Bird.* Bert Stiles left college to enlist in the Army Air Force, flew as copilot on thirty-five bomber missions over France and Germany, won the Air Medal and Distinguished Flying Cross, and then, instead of taking up his leave and returning to the United States, requested transfer to fighters and was shot down in a P-51 over Germany in 1944, at the age of twenty-three.

Returning from a particularly savage mission over Munich one day—as it turned out, very near the end of his life—this young airman and his pilot rode their bicycles out into the English countryside, bought four pounds of strawberries, and while consuming them fell into a long educational colloquy in which our school and college committee will find strong support. I quote the part dealing with secondary education:

I was involved in an outfit called the Progressive Education Group, with forty picked members from the two feeding junior high schools, picked for character and brains and general affability. We stayed together all the way through high school. We were a hot outfit all right . . . two teachers and forty eager beavers on our way to the moon.

The School Board signed away all its powers. We could take a shot at anything, any subject, any whim, for as long or as short as we desired. We could pick our courses and our teachers. We could go on field trips, and use the school bus. We could do anything we chose, for two hours of the school day. The first year it was three hours a day. Progressive English one hour a day, progressive social science one hour (the names didn't mean anything), and progressive science one hour.

Progressive science turned out to be a spectacular flop and was discontinued. Each member of the class chose some scientific subject to investigate and report on to the others. It took a year to give all the reports.

I chose sleeping bags, and the science of keeping warm in one, and made a gala report on this in April, and just sat there and slept the rest of the year. I think my report had something to do with their discontinuing the course. . . .

I could remember most of the educational byways that class flung itself down . . . a speed-up course in psychology, a quick survey of adolescent sex problems. We started to produce a series of plays and never finished. . . .

We wrote poems and short stories, and seriously

delved into the art of letter writing. We spent one spring learning the stories of operas. We debated whether to spend a little time on history, and decided not.

We spoke extemporaneously. We spoke out of turn. We ranted and raised hell and went out on field trips and took in the key movies, and had a few parties to develop social poise.

When we made our reports at the end, I stated I hadn't gotten a whole hell of a lot out of it.

It is an easy step from these curricular delusions to the corruption of college athletics, which represents yet another symptom of shallow draughts from the Pierian spring. The whole sad, innocent and not so innocent confusion of values that produces such results as the West Point scandal and the basketball fixes; the million dollar gate receipts; the open traffic in football scholarships and "additional compensations" averaging as high in some cases as $3,000 or $4,000 a year; the underground recruitment of football players by alumni and coaches of colleges that frown upon it in principle; the fantastic case histories of athletes majoring in physical education and receiving course credit for football, handball, elementary swimming, social dancing, rhythms, and fly fishing; the seamy double standard spreading through college communities as from a tainted well . . . it is a tale of educational assets mortgaged to the entertainment industry, of educational opportunities squandered in the coliseum, of men content with a little learning and impatient with that if it gets in the way of a winning team.

Do you again suspect me of speaking from the ivory tower? I am uttering the thoughts of sports columnists as well as university presidents, of undergraduates as well as faculty members, of athletes as well as scholars, of athletes who are scholars and of scholars who are athletes. Two years of military service are crowding into the already overcrowded educational years of these young men, with perhaps an *Iliad* or an *Odyssey* lying beyond them, inclining their thoughts more and more to that unfinished business of Bert Stiles.

It is perfectly possible, I would say essential, to find room in these years for active participation in organized athletic sports. I am proud to represent a university in which no fewer than three thousand of its four thousand undergraduates participate in such sports, and I intend to do everything I can to increase rather than diminish this number. I believe this program should continue to include intercollegiate as well as intramural competition. But I also believe that the athletic cloth should be cut to the educational pattern: that intercollegiate competition should be conducted on a single-standard, amateur basis; that individual ethics should be substituted for the group ethics now governing that competition; and that according to these individual ethics it is no more justifiable for a college to recruit football or basketball players by special financial inducements or curricular concessions than it would be for me to inveigle your headmaster into a game of golf and then hire Sam Snead to disguise himself as me and go out and take the headmaster's watch and pocketbook away from him. To condone such practices in the name of education adds moral to intellectual confusion and puts one more delusion in the way of our proper educational goals.

Let me now touch upon a less lurid, though to you gentlemen more insidious and possibly more dangerous delusion. This is the idea that college is an end in itself and that distinction as an undergraduate, particularly social distinction, is the *summum bonum*. Believe me, college is not an end in itself but the means to an end, the preparation for life, not the final experience; and there is no sadder inversion of values than that which sacrifices the preparation for the final experience. You will give this same advice to your sons some day though you may not take it for yourselves, and you will look back on the man who made a career of campus success as Max Beerbohm looks upon the Duke of Dorset in his glittering satire, *Zuleika Dobson*. We find this Oxford paragon at the very peak of his undergraduate career as president of the Junta:

> The Duke had been elected in his second term. At that time there were four members; but these were all leaving Oxford at the end of the summer term, and there seemed to be in the ranks of the Bullingdon and the Loder no one quite eligible for the Junta, that holy of holies. Thus it was that the Duke inaugurated in solitude his second year of membership. From time to time, he proposed and seconded a few candidates . . . but always . . . when election evening . . . drew near, he began to have his doubts about these fellows . . . Election evening was always a rather melancholy time. After dinner, when the two club servants had placed on the mahogany the time-worn Candidates' Book and the ballot-box, and had noiselessly withdrawn, the Duke, clearing his throat, read aloud to himself "Mr. So-and-So, of Such-and-Such College, proposed by the Duke of Dorset, seconded by the Duke of Dorset,"

> and in every case, when he drew out the drawer of the ballot-box, found it was a black-ball that he had dropped into the urn. Thus it was that at the end of the summer term the annual photographic "group" taken by Messrs. Hills and Saunders was a presentment of the Duke alone.

The Duke symbolizes the end result of a process that costs many an undergraduate precious educational opportunities and leaves him, soon after graduation, in greater loneliness than even the Duke knew.

Is learning safe? That is a question we often hear nowadays, and there are some Americans who have concluded in the negative. Our schools and colleges are accused of subversive activities, textbooks are banned, teachers are suspected for what they do and say not merely as individual citizens but as members of their profession. If a little learning is dangerous, a lot of learning is much more dangerous. It will destroy our faith and make us traitors to our country.

I believe that the people who talk this way prove better than any evidence I have offered here that Alexander Pope was right. Books won't stay banned. They won't burn. Ideas won't go to jail. In the long run of history, the censor and the inquisitor have always lost. The only sure weapon against bad ideas is better ideas. The source of better ideas is wisdom. The surest path to wisdom is a liberal education.

The cold war is the great fact of our day. It is a war of ideas. What folly it is to suppose that the schoolboy who hears and sees discussions of these ideas on radio and television, in the newspapers and magazines on his living-room table, or in the books in his local bookstores and library, is being protected from them by not mentioning them in the classroom. The whole genius and strength of democracy is epitomized by the man who prefers the better because he understands the worse. He is the perfect embodiment of the liberal education for which this Academy stands. It is not in countries where this type of education has flourished that communism has made progress but in countries where great ignorant masses of peasants were denied even a little learning. Communism itself, with its philosophical pretensions and its double talk, its captive science and literature, is the full flower of a little learning. Is not the obvious defense against it those deeper draughts prescribed by Pope, prohibited in Russia, yet still permissible in the United States? Is it not contorted logic to believe that liberal education, which the Kremlin fears (and therefore prohibits) will be the death of communism in Russia, will be the birth of it in the United States?

You will hear it said, finally, that there is too much learning, that when people get too well educated they won't want to work. Work at what? The learned professions? In these, work and education and satisfaction are synonymous. Work in industry? With their high wages and their 40-hour week, what will our factory workers do with their other 128 hours? Allowing 56 for sleep and 21 for meals, that still leaves 51 in which education might prove itself. What else will fill these hours? Television? Movies? Demagogues? A little learning? Often you will find that the man who argues too much education occupies the same cultural level as the man to whom he applies the argument. The minute he steps out of his office he steps into the same car, the same movie show, the same television program, the same sleepy evening; reads the same newspapers and magazines, drinks the same beer, smokes the same cigarettes, listens to the same radio broadcasts. Observing these two gentlemen in their use of leisure time, a man from another planet might conclude that their educational advantages had been identical. This is an infirm foundation, is it not, for the curtailment of these advantages to either. We all live in the same country, under the same government. We are all responsible for choosing this government and for understanding and judging its policies. We believe in equal opportunity. The proof of equal opportunity is mobility. The key to mobility is education. The idea that there can be too much education is all very well for a feudal system or a dictatorship, but it is a contradiction in terms in a democracy.

Gentlemen of Andover, your Academy was founded in the year 1778. This was a critical year in the history of our country. It is true that just the year before we had won the Battle of Saratoga and Benjamin Franklin had then signed certain treaties of commerce and alliance with France. But Washington was at Valley Forge and the British held New York and Philadelphia.

I will give you two propositions for the year 1778: a little learning was a dangerous thing, and so was being an American. It is to your everlasting credit that for over a century and three-quarters, in the forefront of American education, your Academy has, with flawless logic, inspired teaching, and liberal learning, proved the first proposition and disproved the second. May you continue to do so, to the common benefit of American education and American democracy.

Baccalaureate Address

(Second annual sermon to Yale seniors,

June 8, 1952)

> For unto whom much is given, of him shall be much required: and to whom men have committed much, of him they will ask the more.
>
> ST. LUKE 12:48

With this Commencement we bring to a close the observance of our 250th year as college and university. It has been a year for reflection. A world preoccupied with other things, indifferent, often hostile, to higher learning, has tested our first principles and purposes. Great acts of charity have been performed in support of those purposes. Scholars from all parts of the free world have paid tribute to them, exhorted us to hold fast to them, pledged us their faith for the future. A year ago on this occasion I was concerned with the opportunities that the future holds for us as individuals. Today I am concerned with the corollary, the responsibilities we must assume if we are to realize those opportunities. In keeping with our anniversary, I would direct our thoughts to the responsibilities we owe our schools and universities. They have given us much: they require much of us. Their welfare is in our hands: the more faithful we are to this trust the more it will ask of us.

Opportunity and responsibility—in the combination we have the cardinal principle, the gyrostabilizer, of democracy. I wish our Commencement ceremonies put more stress on this principle. The medieval context surviving in these gowns and hoods survives, too, in the phrasing of our academic diplomas. This, as you will see, admits each candidate upon whom a degree is conferred "to all its rights and privileges." I wish instead it admitted him "to all its responsibilities." I have two hard-earned degrees from Yale and several honorary ones from other institutions, and for the life of me I cannot tell you how to enjoy this Magna Charta of rights and privileges. But I can tell you something about the opportunities represented by those degrees and a great deal more about the responsibilities. With its note of finished business culminating in mystical elevation, our bachelor's degree reads like a vaccination certificate as preamble to a fraternal order. I wish it read more like *Pilgrim's Progress.*

We have a long, hard way to go if we are to enable American education to realize its ideals and perform the functions expected of it in our society. You have heard much of the troubles of our educational system this year —of a financial crisis affecting both public and private institutions, the seriousness of which will have to be felt yet more painfully, apparently, before it is generally understood; of appalling shortages of school teachers; of overloaded and ill-disciplined school rooms; of political trends that threaten the independence and impair the usefulness of the educational process; of educational assets mortgaged to the entertainment industry; of popular delusions identifying higher learning with immorality and treason. These troubles are monstrous things that grow more monstrous at close range and in the heat of controversy. How can we be delivered from them?

There is no lack of prescriptions for the needs of American education. But while the doctors argue the patient grows sicker, at all events fails to improve, and the prognosis remains gloomy. We are baffled by symptoms, symptoms of a youthful society that does not understand itself, that does not know the power of its ideals or the strength of its institutions. We are the descendants of men who, the moment they set foot upon these shores posted ignorance as the playground of evil; who in 1647, to forestall the works of "that old deluder, Satan," and in order "that learning may not be buried in the grave of our fathers in the Church and Commonwealth," adopted the first general education act in history; who founded nine colleges before even achieving their independence, who, upon achieving that independence, again proscribed ignorance as the domain of despots and dedicated themselves to education as the safeguard of liberty and the prerequisite of self-government; who since those early times have led the world in bringing educational opportunities to their fellow citizens in fulfillment of the democratic promise. We are proud of our schools and colleges. We eagerly desire education for our children. Yet we do not, as a people, understand its fundamental value. Once we did we would discover the means and no less surely evolve the methods for restoring it to vigor.

To carry this understanding far and wide through our society, to teach it by example and to strengthen it by good works, these are the true "rights and privileges" to which our academic degrees admit us: to make our countrymen understand the difference between man the animal and man the mind and soul; between the world with Shakespeare in it and the world with him left out. But even we, here in this room, may be assailed by doubts. The goal is noble, we may say, but how can we possibly achieve it? It is so expensive, so far, so fraught with controversy; how can our individual efforts count? There was a time in the world's history when the merest handful of individuals preserved the learning and with it the continuity of western civilization; when barbarians who had no conception of the value of learning all but obliterated it from the face of the earth. A knowledge of what befell western Europe in the Dark Ages might resolve our doubts. It might give us a better idea of what we have to lose, hence what we have to preserve, than any amount of argument from contemporary premises.

When in the year 476 the Roman Empire, under the combined stress of invasion from without and corruption within, finally collapsed, civilization in western Europe was not merely arrested. It was reversed. As time moved forward it moved backward until in a hundred years or so it had reverted to where it had stood in the Homeric age, around 1000 B.C. Nor is this a full measure of the setback. In science and the arts and in many other respects European civilization did not regain the heights to which the Greeks and Romans had carried it until the Renaissance of the fifteenth century, adding another millennium to its total loss.

For five hundred of these years, roughly from 500 to 1000 A.D., western Europeans groped and scavenged and fought one another in a state of savagery. Though a few sparks of learning survived, more by chance than by design, in monasteries and cathedral cloisters, outside their walls light retreated before almost total darkness. People forgot how to read. Writing became so uncommon it was regarded as magic. Greek and Latin, science, art, literature, philosophy, all were forgotten. Wild tribesmen swarmed over Hadrian's wall and drove their longboats across the North Sea to subjugate Roman Britain. Huts appeared where villas had stood; campfires burned over the ruins of public buildings, the rule of law gave way to piratical raids and tribal warfare. Continental Europe became a wilderness of ruins, crude forts, and primitive villages separated by vast backwoods areas inhabited by savages.

I wonder if all this would have happened if there had been universities in the ancient world, buttressed and supported by such a comprehensive system of primary and secondary education as our own and animated by similar ideals. It is not for us to rewrite *The Decline and Fall of the Roman Empire*. But may we not, for such moral instruction as it may afford us, indulge in this speculation? There were no universities in the Roman Empire and only a few schools of rhetoric and eloquence. The learning was there, the arts and philosophy of the Greeks; the majestic code of Roman law; the spiritual impulse of Jews and Christians; Vergil and Cicero carrying on the tradition of Homer, Plato, and Aristotle. When the empire was at its height this learning was widespread and respected. But when the drought came it lacked institutional roots to sustain it. It was able neither to arrest the decline nor to prevent the fall, barely able to save its own life in the years that followed.

It may stretch the point to suppose that a thriving system of education might have written a different chapter of history. Yet consider the circumstances of Rome's downfall. All around the distended frontiers of the empire stood the barbarians, ready to take advantage of any cracks, any flaws, any signs of weakness. They might yet have been withstood had it not been for conditions inside the empire. Here economic stupidity and political repression, moral degeneracy, cultural decay, a pervasive corruption of public spirit, a debilitating materialism, all herald and speed the debacle; all come within the meaning of the word ignorance; all respond to education. Instead of education the people were offered distraction, in games and spectacles and holidays that rose to the number of 175 a year, and as these spectacles grew more depraved, so did their onlookers. Meantime the men who governed them, the emperors who witnessed the decline and were engulfed in the fall, lived in hiding in Constantinople and Ravenna, prisoners of the palace, surrounded by spies and sycophants, drowning in intrigue, dying by assassination. Suppose the Roman people and their leaders had been taught to read and write, steeped in the liberal arts, instructed in law and history. Might they not have seen, and stopped, the inner decay that weakened their resistance to the barbarians?

Again, when the collapse did come, might not schools and universities have saved western civilization from such a long and nearly fatal sleep? As it was, that civilization escaped death by the slimmest of margins—because monks continued to illuminate and thus save the life of manuscripts; because single copies of ancient literary and scientific works were overlooked in dusty corners and so preserved from destruction; because song schools continued to teach Latin not as the key to learning but in order that chants might continuc to bc sung in cathedrals; because Arab traders revealed a knowledge of the ancients, not as pedagogy but as gossip in the market place; because a few churchmen kept up their reading, and one or two bold spirits like the Venerable Bede even took to writing. It was a very near thing. When with the founding of the first universities in the twelfth century the revival of learning really began, it was a rediscovery of lost treasures rather than a creation of new ones. The truly creative process had to wait for the Renaissance. If the universities had existed from the beginning, would the sleep have been so deep and the awakening so slow?

I raise these questions not to reinterpret history but to suggest the value of education in our own lifetime. The barbarians stand upon our frontiers. We, too, suffer from distraction and corruption, to the peril of our minds and souls and the ultimate peril of our civilization. But whereas education lacked roots to sustain it against these evils in the fifth century, it has deep roots, in our schools and colleges and universities today.

Gentlemen of the graduating class: the way you tend those roots will determine whether we shall have the best of two worlds, the Graeco-Roman—and our own; or the worst. Either is possible. The choice is up to you. If you neglect those roots, or despise them, they will wither. If you tend them well they will be our surest guarantee that the intellectual and spiritual force imparted to western civilization by the Greeks and Romans —all that Homer meant to Vergil and Vergil to Dante; all that classic tragedy meant to Shakespeare and Milton; all that Aristotle meant to Aquinas, to Hooker and Locke and the Anglo-American political tradition; all this striving to transcend the animal kingdom; all this life of the mind and "bread for the soul" will not again suffer an interruption that was almost an extinction. You do not leave this responsibility behind you when you leave this university. You assume it. It is the unwritten clause in your diploma that validates the whole contract. "For unto whom much is given, of him shall be much required: and to whom men have committed much, of him they will ask the more."

Report to the Alumni, 1951-52

(Second annual report, December, 1952)

In my first report to the alumni a year ago I was chiefly concerned with the external circumstances, especially the economic circumstances, affecting the welfare and prospects of the University. Because of the continuing importance of this subject and the necessity of seeing it in relation to all the University's particular interests and activities, I propose to continue the discussion in this report.

There is a time for everything. There is a time for taking stock of our accomplishments and a time for measuring the resources that make those accomplishments possible. This is a time when the best interests of Yale and of all similar private institutions of higher education require that they look to their resources. For these can no longer be taken for granted, either in quantity or in kind. Institutional plans and policies that do not face this fact are unrealistic, to say the least. The fact itself places a gigantic question mark against the future of American education.

I return, therefore, to the fateful question of our resources. If we have reason to be proud of our past accomplishments, we have all the greater reason for concern with the means of sustaining them and carrying them forward into the future. It is a common occurrence these days for meetings of university presidents to open with exciting prospects of new educational worlds to conquer and close with despairing prophecies of insolvency. This is not a healthy frame of mind. It is very different from the mood in which Yale was founded. The Founders never doubted their purposes or the means of society to support those purposes. Today many a university president is so doubtful of the means of society to support his institution that he becomes doubtful of its purposes, or feels compelled to question them against his will, and is tempted to depart from pure learning for more "profitable" ventures that may enable his institution to survive.

Educational standards suffer when teachers and scholars are contracted out of teaching and scholarship into *ad hoc,* utilitarian projects in the hope of temporary income. They suffer when the supposedly more profitable, because decidedly more marketable, vocational curriculum makes inroads upon the liberal arts. They suffer when they are discounted in exchange for athletes whose prowess is exploited as a source of institutional revenue. All these things are happening in American higher education, to its great disadvantage and ultimate peril, partly, it is true, because of its immaturity and confused values, but partly also, and in growing measure, because of its desperate need for resources.

They are not yet happening at Yale. I hope they never will. But they are happening in the United States much too frequently and over much too wide an area to give

Yale comfort. Obviously, Yale depends on other schools and colleges for her essential raw material. For our undergraduates we depend on the secondary schools and for a large share of our graduate and professional students on other colleges and universities. If the raw material is not forthcoming, if it cannot meet our standards or *will* not meet them because it has been seduced by easier ones, what then?

At the moment those standards are under heavy pressure, part of which is the sheer weight of numbers, part of which is organized and deliberate. In both cases the public institutions bear a disproportionate share of the pressure and the private institutions a disproportionate share of the responsibility for resisting it. The private institutions must find the resources equal to the task, which for Yale, if she would maintain her leadership, means far more than her numerical average. This is a Yale interest that is also a national interest.

I doubt that many of us appreciate either the nature or the extent of the pressures under which our public institutions are laboring. Not only are the state universities facing increasingly severe competition from other state agencies and functions, particularly highways and public health, in securing their share of state income; but within their own orbit their resources are being heavily strained by the demands of the public schools. These schools enroll over 90 per cent of the nation's entire school population. They are the source of over 95 per cent of the students attending the state universities. Some states require by law that the graduates of accredited public high schools within the state be admitted to the state university by school graduation certificate, and even in the absence of such legislation the moral obligation of the university to admit them on this basis is strong. Thus both the financial and the educational conditions obtaining within the public schools in each state impose direct and serious limitations upon its institutions of higher education.

And what are the conditions within the public schools? They are conditions that reflect our failure as a nation to keep abreast of the increase in our population in the provision of essential school facilities. At their worst in metropolitan and rural areas, at their best in suburban, they are conditions of overcrowded classrooms, of lack of discipline, of underpaid and too often unqualified teachers, that are exacting a heavy toll from American society. By the fall of 1957 it is estimated that our total school population will reach 32,000,000, an increase of 6,000,000 from 1951. To provide for this adequately, new buildings, replacements, and renovations amounting to 600,000 new schoolrooms will be necessary, at an estimated cost of $16,000,000,000. To staff these rooms a quota of 130,000 new teachers per year for the next ten years will be required, and to ensure the quality of this staff substantial increases in teachers' salaries will have to be accomplished throughout the nation.

How much the total bill will come to is anybody's guess. But it is no guess that it will increase the competition for public funds in which public higher education is already involved and that until the minimal needs represented by the bill are provided they will continue to undermine the standards of public higher education.

This is why I have termed our own preservation of standards a Yale interest that is also a national interest. We too depend on the public schools—for upward of 40 per cent of our undergraduates—as does every private college and university in greater or less degree. But we are not pitted against them in such circumscribed and intensive competition for funds as are the state universities, and we admit their graduates on the same terms as private-school graduates, by College Board entrance examinations and other tests, that is to say, by standards fixed by ourselves rather than by the schools. It is these fundamental facts rather than pride of place or tradition that show us our responsibility. It is these pragmatic considerations of the general welfare that urge upon Yale the importance of maintaining educational standards.

Much the same considerations may be applied to the role of private initiative in higher education. If it should disappear here, at this vital and pervasive cultural source, I do not see how it can fail to disappear everywhere else in our society. We have resolved as a nation that it shall not disappear everywhere else. We have pledged ourselves to the mixed polity of Aristotelian principle and democratic tradition, in which authority is divided and diffused and private initiative flourishes in healthy competition with public. We have, as I have frequently pointed out, categorically included higher education in this pledge. The pledge has yet to be translated into policy.

As I reported last year, barely 10 per cent of our annual expenditures on higher education in the United States in 1900 was public in origin. Today the proportion is over 50, is increasing, and is expected in some quarters to go to 75 or 80 per cent. It is often assumed that in Great Britain, where the proportions of public and private funds annually expended on higher education are roughly 65 per cent public and 35 per cent private, public initiative in higher education has expanded much farther than in the United States. The fact is that if the financial resources of our private institutions continue to dwindle, the private share in American higher education may become smaller than in British. This is a point that is often missed by British proponents of the university grants system and one that does not show up in comparisons of the financial structure of Yale with that of Oxford and Cambridge. Their income is 66 per cent public; ours is over 90 per cent private. But our high private percentage merely goes to weight a national average which is already not far from the British and which, if our percentage shrank very much, would probably rise above the British. Yale's financial fortunes would not of themselves cause this to happen; but they are part of Harvard's, Princeton's, and Columbia's. If ours deteriorate, so will theirs, and the result will be as I have conjectured it.

In the light of these considerations I am glad to be able to report some hopeful signs and some solid and most encouraging accomplishments. Among the hopeful signs are an upward revision of the federal income tax exemption for individual contributions to charity from 15 to 20 per cent. While this falls a long way short of ensuring our private institutions in general or Yale in particular their necessary share of income from private charity, it at least shows a recognition of their problem on the part of Congress and a willingness to treat it as a legitimate item of national interest. It also shows the effectiveness of the Association of American Universities, of which Yale is a member, and which includes both public and private institutions, in bringing their common interests to the attention of Congress. We may well hope that it will be followed by further steps toward a comprehensive public policy that will enable both groups of institutions to thrive.

Related developments of no less potential benefit to Yale have taken place in the corporate field. Here, as I indicated in my last report and as others have demonstrated in detail, the financial resources of our corporations—the greatest of all reservoirs of private wealth in our society—that might be made available to our universities are backed up behind a log jam of legal and administrative obstacles that permits only a faint trickle to escape. In 1949, for example, our corporations showed a net income before taxes of $28,300,000,000. Under their 5 per cent tax exemption, this permitted them $1,400,000,000 to spend on charities of all kinds. Actually they spent only $223,000,000, under 8/10 of 1 per cent of their net taxable income. How much of this went to our private colleges and universities may be deduced from the fact that in 1950 71 per cent of the total corporate contribution went to welfare and health agencies, and only 21 per cent to education. Since this latter category included education of all types, the share of higher education must be reduced in proportion and the share of the private institutions in that share reduced still further. By this process it has been estimated that in 1949–50 the private colleges and universities received in corporate gifts a total of only $10,000,000. Against current expenditures of $600,000,000, this was hardly more than a drop in the bucket.

Still it was a very significant, hopeful drop. For it represented a stirring of interest among the leaders of American business and industry in the financial circumstances of our colleges and universities. Further signs of this interest were:

1. The growing number of business and industrial executives who have publicly espoused the cause of corporate support for higher education.

2. The rapidly expanding literature on the subject, with prominent mention of the studies already published or in process of publication by the National Planning Association, the Russell Sage Foundation, and the Commission on Financing Higher Education.

3. The fact that, by January 1952 twenty-six states had enacted legislation permitting corporate giving.

4. The spreading corporate practice of establishing charitable foundations and trusts such as the Ford Motor Company Fund in Dearborn and the H. J. Heinz Company Foundation in Pittsburgh.

5. The progress of the National Fund for Medical Education. Founded in 1949 for the purpose of interpreting the needs of medical education, improving its standards, and providing it financial resources, the fund's receipts for distribution to the nation's medical schools rose from \$183,700 in 1949–50 to \$1,300,000 in 1951 and \$1,500,000 for the first ten months of 1952. The potential importance of this fund is great not only to the field of medical education but, as an example, to higher education in general.

6. The Ford Motor Company's scholarship program for children of its employees, and others like it. The Ford program takes specific account of the needs of the private institutions by granting any such institution selected by one of its scholarship recipients \$500 in excess of tuition.

7. The Yale scholarship recently established by Sargent and Company of New Haven, which, like the Ford, is awarded competitively to children of its employees and includes room and board as well as tuition, but which

also represents a growing trend of corporate support for higher education on a local basis.

8. The fact that, whatever the size of their contributions to the private colleges and universities, our corporations are currently giving to charity eight times as much as they gave before the war.

9. The consensus among both corporation executives and stockholders, as attested by numerous studies, interviews, and polls, that education should and will receive a larger share of corporate earnings, not only through scholarship programs but also through direct grants.

10. The founding in New York of the Council for Financial Aid to Education, Inc., whose purposes are stated as follows:

> To promote a better understanding by the managers and owners of American business, foundations and other organizations, whether incorporated or otherwise, and by the members of the public, of the substantial contribution which higher education has made and is making to the effectiveness and to the development of this country, and to aid in bringing about a recognition by the managers and owners of American business, foundations and other organizations, whether incorporated or otherwise, and by the members of the public, of the importance to American business and to the nation as a whole of securing adequate financial support of higher education in this country, particularly through contributions and aid from American business concerns, foundations, labor unions and other organizations, whether incorporated or otherwise, as well as from members of the public.

> To serve in an advisory and coöperative capacity, both to prospective contributors and to educational institutions, in connection with the formulation, adoption and carrying out of programs of various kinds having for their general purpose the obtaining of financial support in one form or another for educational institutions in this country, and to further, by the dissemination of information and otherwise, programs having that objective . . . the corporation is not itself to distribute funds to educational institutions or to solicit contributions for such purpose.

By keeping itself free of the pressures and administrative detail involved in the solicitation and distribution of funds the council has enormously improved its chances of achieving its stated purposes. If it should achieve those purposes, it will have performed one of the greatest services to American education in our generation.

These are all hopeful signs. Notwithstanding the legal barriers to more substantial corporate giving, which are now under study and in test litigation, three things seem clear. One is that our corporations have it within their power to bring about a dramatic improvement in the financial fortunes of our colleges and universities, particularly our private colleges and universities. The second is that there is a disposition on the part of both corporation executives and stockholders to do exactly that. The third is that this disposition must be galvanized by intellectual conviction before it becomes policy and practice.

There can be little doubt of the potential. The executive director of the Commission on Financing Higher

Education has estimated that if the corporations had brought their charitable contributions up to 3 per cent of net taxable income for 1949–50 and the share of higher education in these contributions up to 25 per cent, the resulting income for the latter would have been $325,-000,000; and that if $200,000,000 of this had been allocated to the private colleges and universities, it would have represented one-third of their total income for that year. The potential is there. The urge to use it is widespread. All that is lacking is the conviction that this must be done.

I turn now from hopeful signs to solid accomplishments. In 1951–52 our Alumni Fund for the second successive year broke all records for funds of its type. It raised a total of $1,015,418 from 24,242 alumni and parents. In cash the gift is equivalent to the income from $25,000,000 in carefully invested endowment. This sum brought the gross amount of all funds donated to Yale for all purposes during the year to $14,111,707.

All but a small proportion of this total (14 per cent) was individual, private charity, most of it bestowed upon the University by its own alumni. Much of this can be credited to the devoted services of Alumni Fund agents, much to the effectiveness of our alumni organizations as a whole. All of it can be credited to the generosity of the donors, and all of it was given not out of sentiment alone but in proof of the maxim that "real excellence is most recognized when most openly looked into."

Charity of this sort has been the mainstay of Yale since Elihu Yale's original gift. With all the odds that militate against it and whittle down its value today, it is still Yale's margin between progress and retrenchment—we might as well say between success and failure. Why should this be so? We are doing well now; why keep trying to do better? Because only by trying to do better shall we continue to do as well. This is a truism in the life of institutions as it is in the life of individuals. In the life of individuals it represents the chief difference between men and apes. In the life of Yale it represents the essential self-criticism and creative effort that have earned us our present place of honor—and of responsibility—among the universities of the world.

How difficult it is for us to keep up that effort may be judged from the fact that, from 1940 to 1952, while our endowment increased 22 per cent our operating costs rose more than 100 per cent—a little over four times the rate of increase of our endowment. We have striven for all possible economies. We submitted the entire non-academic operating plant of the University to outside, professional analysis, on the strength of which substantial economies were effected. We have increased our tuition charges to the maximum deemed feasible in relation to the charges of other institutions. Our program of student aid is under study by a Corporation committee. We have pruned our educational budget to what our faculties regard as a minimum consistent with our educational standards and what I must conscientiously report to the alumni as below the optimum.

This is true everywhere we look. We are caught in a secular trend of rising costs, and our income from all sources fails to catch up with them. We are not contemplating expansion. Quite the opposite, we are trying to reduce the size of our present student body and for the first time since the war have actually succeeded in applying this policy to the present freshman class. Expansion is not the cause of our troubles. We are merely trying to stay in business and keep up the quality of our product. We are bursting at the seams not because we have outgrown our suit of clothes but because we have outworn it.

Our best hope of putting this situation to rights remains individual private charity. The foundations will not do it for us. Their total resources are too small and the pressures upon them too great for undertakings of this kind. Their combined contribution to the total cost of higher education in the United States barely exceeds 2 per cent, and to Yale's income 3 per cent. This contribution is made in the form of term grants which, however helpful, indeed invaluable, as pump primers and venture capital, invariably turn into net increases in costs to their recipients rather than net increments to operating funds or capital account. Moreover, the grants are made for specific projects which sometimes represent the educational plans of the grantor more faithfully than they do the educational needs of the recipient and which, however meritorious, add nothing to our small store of unrestricted funds.

The same is true of the present corporate contribution to higher education. The small corporate contribution which now finds its way into higher education is so narrowly restricted to *quid pro quo* arrangements that its benefits to general education are minimal and the possibility of using it to eke out operating funds practically nil. It has a long educational process to undergo before it gets beyond vocational training and technology into the main arteries of higher education.

How can we expedite this process? How can we help one another perceive as corporate executives and stockholders, as voters and as congressmen, the things we seem better able to perceive as individual taxpayers and alumni? This is the question before the house. I put the question thus because the alumni of Yale have perceived the needs of their University so clearly and have rallied so strongly in its support that I could hope for nothing better for Yale—or for American higher education—than that their perception be projected into corporate practice and public policy.

This would ensure the resources we need and all that hinges upon them: the high educational standards, the private initiative, and the democratic polity, not just at Yale but throughout the United States. Meanwhile, as Yale has given a good account of herself in American education for two hundred and fifty years, and as her alumni have given a good account of themselves as private citizens and in the nation's affairs, we shall continue, with whatever resources we may have, trying to do better in order that we may continue to do as well.

The Liberal Arts at Midcentury

(Address at the University of Georgia, March 6, 1953)

When you did me the honor of inviting me to address you on the liberal arts at midcentury, I am glad you did not specify what century this was to be. If you had specified the twentieth century, I should undoubtedly have found myself repeating words of wisdom spoken on this subject in these very halls at the Conference on Liberal Arts you held here a year ago. If you had specified some other century, I might have found myself at a loss for the connecting link between that century and our own. As it is my title leaves us conveniently up in the air, high enough up, I hope, for a cosmic view in which Yale and the University of Georgia, the medieval universities from which they sprang, the ancient Greeks and the present and future citizens of the United States form one timeless unity of purpose and principle. In deference to our common Connecticut ancestors, I invoke the mood of the Connecticut Yankee in King Arthur's Court. But I charge that Yankee with more serious business than out-carpetbagging the carpetbaggers among the chivalrous cohorts of King Arthur.

It is my thesis here today that the liberal arts are in deadly peril, not only in our own country but in the countries of their origin; and that if they are to be saved and restored to influence in our civilization, it will take a mighty effort on the part of the schools and colleges and universities in all those countries, but especially in the United States. In this, as in every other cultural task, the part of the world that is under the domination of Russian communism is lost to us at least for the time being; and the part that is free stands too much in dread of that domination, is too much preoccupied with the national economic and political reconstruction necessary to keep out from under it, to give us help. The sun of the free world rises in the West. This world looks to us for cultural as well as political leadership. I can think of no more effective way for us to supply that leadership than by restoring the liberal arts to their proper and proportionate role in our educational system.

I remember a cartoon I once saw depicting an American archaeologist leaning on his shovel at the bottom of an excavation in Central or South America, with a bemused Indian, in poncho and sombrero, comfortably perched on the rim looking down at him. The American has asked the Indian what he is thinking about, and the Indian replies, "Me think someday maybe we dig you up." The moral of this cartoon haunts me. Suppose that Indian, as leader of the Inca Geographical Society's Archaeological Expedition to the United States, were digging away in the soil above our heads right now—not over Athens or New Haven, please God, but over some kitchen midden of contemporary American culture.

What would he find among the oxidized juke boxes and television sets and the petrified bubble gum?

"Is Americanism a future worth striving for?" asks a former German fighter pilot shot down over Stalingrad, taken prisoner by the Russians, converted to communism, disillusioned, wishing to cast his lot with the West, yet hesitating for want of something to believe in. "Haven't pursuit of the dollar, the conveyor belt, skyscrapers, crime thrillers, the jazz mania done more to demoralize the world and turn man into a mass creature than could a collectivist party dictatorship inspired by a socialist ideal? Where is the towering cultural achievement of America?" *

The question shocks us. We are relieved to learn that the young German finally answered it by escaping to the American zone, renouncing communism, filling the void left by both fascism and communism with hope "that mankind would one day rediscover its conscience and its soul and faith in those values which lie beyond the reach of a secret police": and we file his book away as one more proof of the rightness of our cause. Yet millions of men and women who suffer in bondage on one side of the iron curtain and in fear of bondage on the other are asking themselves the same question as I speak these words. They look to us as the children of Israel looked to Moses. But when the children of Israel looked to Moses they could see the Ten Commandments.

We are the world's greatest salesmen, yet we cannot talk about our greatest product, our democracy. Why should this be so? Is it not because we do not know ourselves? We know a great deal about ourselves, more facts

* Heinrich von Einsiedel, *I Joined the Russians* (Yale University Press, 1953).

and figures than any people ever knew in history. Everybody tells us about ourselves, commentators, publicists, novelists, statisticians, economists, sociologists, analysts, psychoanalysts, everybody. We are the best informed generation that ever lived, with the most primitive ideas of what to do with our information. We know how to blow up the world, but we don't know how to govern it. What is the cause of all this truncated knowledge, this astigmatic vision, this inarticulateness? "There are two sentences inscribed upon the Delphic oracle," says Plutarch, "hugely accommodated to the uses of man's life: 'Know thyself' and 'Nothing too much'; and upon these all other precepts depend." We have neglected the first precept in our national passion and aptitude for the second. It has carried us far. It will carry us no farther without the first.

How may we know ourselves so that we may know our weakness as well as our strength; so that we may understand the relationship between our cultural responsibilities and the political and military objectives to which we are committed; so that we may proclaim the virtues of American life in the universal language of humanity? The question leads straight to the liberal arts. These studies made their appearance in formal education in Greece, more than two thousand years ago. Plato and Aristotle both recognized their vital role in the education of the ideal citizen. There is much misunderstanding as to the meaning of the term "liberal arts." It means, and has meant from the beginning, the arts or studies becoming to a free man. Their purpose in our educational system was well stated by John Stuart Mill when he said it was to make "capable and cultivated human beings. . . . Men are men before they are lawyers or physicians or manufacturers; and if you make them capable and sensible men, they will make themselves capable and sensible lawyers or physicians."

Mill spoke these words in his inaugural address as rector of St. Andrews University, Scotland. In his *Autobiography* he sums up the purpose of the address in a passage that I think holds much wisdom for us here today. He was not praising the liberal arts in order to attack the sciences. His position, he says, was "to vindicate the high educational value alike of the old classics and the new scientific studies" and to insist "that it is only the stupid inefficiency of the usual teaching which makes those studies be regarded as competitors instead of allies."

This is not only a good statement of the purpose of the liberal arts but a sound conception of their place in education. Mill says they are vital, not exclusive. So I would say today. The *trivium* (grammar, rhetoric, and logic) and *quadrivium* (arithmetic, geometry, astronomy, and music) of the medieval curriculum have broadened to include such studies as language, literature, philosophy, the fine arts, and history. These subjects can and should be taught in a context that includes the sciences and social studies. I do not suggest shrinking them down to their hard medieval core and offering that as the whole apple. My point is that in our national educational system they have already shrunk to a brown and seedy core which the janitor has picked up and is about to drop in the wastebasket, and that unless we rescue this and plant it and cultivate it, its fruit will be lost to a society that desperately needs it.

Do I exaggerate the plight of the liberal arts? Let me take liberty with my title and imagine midcentury to mean the middle of the twelfth century A.D. Suppose we were living then, in foreknowledge of the founding of the first universities that was shortly to follow, and I were addressing you on the same subject as I am today. I should report approximately as follows:

1. The liberal arts are about to play a decisive role in western civilization.
2. Universities will soon be founded at Bologna, Paris, Oxford, and Cambridge.
3. These universities will rescue the learning of the past from oblivion and put it in circulation in western Europe.
4. They will rouse western civilization from the coma of the Dark Ages.
5. They will shape the whole course of medieval thought.
6. They will lay the foundations of modern learning.
7. They will accomplish these things by energetically applying to individual minds the stimulus and discipline of the liberal arts.
8. Therefore, as I have said, the liberal arts are about to play a decisive role in western civilization.

I could give you no such favorable report today. Everywhere in Britain and Europe, as well as in the United States, the liberal arts are in retreat before the sciences and vocational studies of all sorts. A brief educational pilgrimage to Britain, Western Germany, and France last summer soon convinced me that we could no longer count on those countries to keep alive the pure flame of liberal learning they lighted eight centuries ago. While the prestige and influence of Oxford and Cambridge and the Scottish universities are still great, new education acts passed in 1944 and 1945 have committed the United Kingdom to public educational responsibilities that our ancestors assumed in principle in the Massachusetts Bay Colony as early as 1641. For the first time British education is face to face with the problem of numbers. Up to now, less than 9 per cent of the seventeen-year age group have been finishing high school in England and Scotland as compared with over 60 per cent in the United States, and barely a third as many of these have been finishing college. The new British and Scottish education acts may not equalize the proportions but they will certainly increase the British proportion and with it the pressure of numbers on quality that we have had to contend with especially during the last half century. I took some small satisfaction in being able to tell my most hospitable British hosts that here at last was a subject in which we had had a little more experience than they.

Along with this great increase in numbers, which their universities are only just beginning to feel, the British have been suffering from austerity to a degree (and with a fortitude) that is hard for us well-fed Americans to imagine. In other words, while the education acts have created a new economic need of the first magnitude, the country is hard put to it to find the economic resources to meet that need. The prospect is already causing young men and women of talent and ability to shun the teaching profession for more profitable employment. Add to these facts the fascination with science that prevails in Britain as it does here; economic insecurity that drives young people into vocational training or forces their parents to pull them out of school or keep them out of college to exploit their earning power; the fear of war and the demands of military service; and a generally materialistic, here-to-day-and-gone-tomorrow outlook on life, and you can see what the traditional homes of the liberal arts—Oxford, Cambridge, the Scottish universities and the English public schools—are confronted with. It begins to sound familiar, doesn't it?

In Germany, as might be expected, these conditions are many times worse. The liberal arts underwent a new Dark Age under Hitler. Then they suffered the ravages of war. Today, after a quarter century of adversity, a few valiant souls are trying to renew them amid the rubble of bombed-out schools and universities overrun by refugees from the Eastern Zone, with little or no money for books and not much more for teachers' salaries. The great German system of secondary and higher education that so much impressed the world in the nineteenth century, with all its faults and virtues, is a thing of the past. With its regimentation and fierce specialization it was none too friendly to the liberal arts anyway. If good is to come from what is left of it—and I say this with humility—it will be because we give decisive support to the German scholars who have found in our conception of the liberal arts an element that was lacking in their national educational system and who are now striving against great odds to include that element in their plans for educational reconstruction.

In France the liberal arts prosper more by reputation than in reality. Although they continue to occupy an important place in French secondary education, this sphere of influence is limited. The weeding out process begins early in French education and admits only the more gifted students to liberal arts studies in the first place. Among these few the same tradition of specialization in higher education as used to prevail in Germany, and the same demand for scientific and vocational training as exists in Britain, militate against the liberal arts in the universities. In an effort to counteract these trends, the national universities have instituted a year of general education (*propédeutique*) in which students are encouraged to continue the liberal arts studies of the *lycées* before entering upon their professional studies. This is all very well as far as it goes, but it does not go far enough. I was told quite frankly by members of the French Ministry of Education in Paris that students were exercising all their native powers of ingenuity to anticipate their professional studies instead of taking advantage of the purpose for which the new year was intended.

To find the small minority of French students who qualify for liberal arts work seeking ways to avoid or circumvent it is not an encouraging sign. Moreover, France is in the grip of an inflation that makes it necessary for university professors to take on other work, often semiskilled or even unskilled in nature, in order to afford to continue their teaching and research and at the same time support their families. Worst of all, the French are assailed by neurotic moods, finding expression alternately in bravado and fatalism and the synthesis of the two in the bleak philosophy of existentialism. We can no more count on France to save the liberal arts than we can count on Germany.

What then, are we doing to discharge the portentous responsibility that devolves upon ourselves? I have begged my own question. I have said we were neglecting it. I repeat that statement, and I challenge anyone with firsthand knowledge of the curricular practices prevailing generally throughout our secondary schools, colleges, and universities to deny it. With all due apologies and exceptions, and all honor to those exceptions, neglect is a conservative diagnosis.

I have at various times tried to state the reasons for this neglect only to find myself bogged down in explanation. I have tried and failed to account for our national confusion of values that honors Shakespeare as a cultural symbol, but when it comes to studying his plays in school, or even reading them for enjoyment, equates them with bookkeeping and decides in favor of bookkeeping. Somehow or other the liberal arts have acquired the reputation of a luxury, not a necessity, a privilege for the gentleman of leisure but a doubtful asset, even a waste of time, to the working man.

Historically, there is some reason for this conception. Although Plato considered the liberal arts essential in the training of the ideal citizen, we must remember that Plato's ideal citizen was a "guardian," the member of a small ruling caste that presided over a fundamentally undemocratic society resting upon a foundation of slavery. Thus when the Greeks proclaimed the liberal arts to mean the arts becoming to a free man, they really meant a privileged man, a man of property and leisure, for only he was truly free in Greek society.

The same was generally true in the Middle Ages, when the liberal arts were revived and infused into western civilization by the first universities. In those days European and English society resembled Athenian society—not Plato's totalitarian blueprint of it but its actual structure of caste and class. Within this structure, economic conditions as well as social philosophy put fetters on all but a small handful—aristocrats, clergy, and indigent scholars—who could benefit from the arts becoming to a free man. Thus the liberal arts became identified as a privilege for the few rather than an opportunity for the many, and this tradition dies hard both in Britain and in Europe.

What truth does it hold for us in the United States? None. We rejected it at the outset. In American history, in the light of our national ideals and the first principles of our democracy, it is heresy. The cardinal principle of our whole democratic government, society, and way of life is equal opportunity. Notwithstanding the limitations imposed upon them by the political philosophy of Plato or the economic and social conditions prevailing in ancient Greece or medieval France and England, intrinsically the liberal arts have been recognized and sought after for two thousand years as the richest educational opportunity of the ideal citizen—as the stimulus and discipline of the mind that best fits it for individual responsibility, that gives it the greatest general competence upon which to draw for the specific competence required in any calling, any profession or vocation, any duty of a citizen in a self-governing society.

It follows, does it not, that the freer the society the greater the responsibilities it imposes upon the individual citizen and the greater these responsibilities, the greater that citizen's need for the help of the liberal arts. Shall we then deny this help to the students in our schools and colleges to whom we promise equal educational as we do equal social opportunity? To do so would be to go back on our own first principles, on our first educational laws and institutions, on the charters of Yale and the University of Georgia.

These laws and institutions were conceived in the spirit of democracy that we find it so hard to describe today, a spirit that places the man ahead of his calling, that seeks to expand to the utmost the only true source of virtue and intelligence in society—not just our society but any society—the conscience and mind of the individual. This is our secret weapon in the cold war. This is the unspoken message we have to convey to our friends. This is what a powerful revival of the liberal arts in our schools and colleges could make available to our world before it is blown to bits or buried in dust and in the hands of the archaeologists.

Baccalaureate Address

(Third annual sermon to the "gentlemen of the graduating class," New Haven, June 7, 1953)

> "Then saith he unto them, Render therefore unto Caesar the things which are Caesar's; and unto God the things that are God's."
>
> MATTHEW 22:21

Is this the Silent Generation? Is this the generation whose critics contend it has done with adventure and longs for security and suburban idylls; whose friends assert it seeks in self-containment the inner strength to discharge the gratuitous task of receiver in bankruptcy for the Noisy Generation that begot it; the generation which both friend and critic agree accepts government but does not acknowledge authority? If it is, of what avail this baccalaureate address? You are the members of the graduating class. Custom decrees that authority speak to you on this occasion. Fate obliges me to represent authority. Yet authority is not acknowledged in the first place, and in the second place, as here represented, it is guilty by association with the Noisy Generation. What then shall authority say?

It will assert nothing. After the fashion of the day it will interrogate. First as to reputations and credentials. Are you so silent? Have I not heard your riotous voices in the street? And was my generation merely noisy? Are you sure it was not the blare of our trumpets that first stampeded authority so that you silent shock troops could mop it up, even as Scipio's trumpets stampeded the elephants of Hannibal and gave Rome victory over the Carthaginians? Could it be that our fortissimo and your pianissimo are both parts of the same score?

If you will allow the possibility, I shall ask us both this question. Have we really taken the measure of authority? Or have we merely won a series of minor skirmishes while the main forces of authority have consolidated and drawn themselves up in more formidable array than ever? We have been lions of courage and eagles of independence in such matters as the drinking of cocktails and the wearing of neckties. Between us, it would seem, we have transformed the home from a patriarchy into a matriarchy, and you are now putting the matriarchy to the supreme test. We flushed the deans. You have treed them. But while we have been winning these triumphs over authority in home and college, authority has been growing in another form—a form so strange to our generation that we scarcely credited its existence but one that has become so familiar to your generation that you take it for granted—the form of the state. We have not even come to terms with this authority.

The growth of the state throughout the world has been a commonplace of our times. First in Russia, then in Italy and Germany, then receding from western Europe but spreading into China, the tide of totalitarian dictatorship seems to have been continuously at the flood. For nearly fifteen years—roughly three-quarters of your lives—our country has been in a condition of full or partial mobilization, for seven years actually at war, to keep this flood from our shores. Meanwhile the free nations have themselves experienced remarkable accretions in the power of the state. Not only those nations whose history and traditions were less democratic, but also Great Britain, and the United States, the two nations whose intimately related political and social institutions form the very vertebrae of modern democracy, have all seen public enterprise move into many areas heretofore occupied by private. To perceive the change in our own case one has but to compare the federal payroll of 1953 with that of 1933, or, for that matter, both major party platforms of 1952 with those of 1932.

A world of difference separates the two kinds of state expansion. While I do not intend to dwell on this difference this morning, neither do I wish to minimize it. I do not see how anyone who understands the Constitution of the United States and the history that brought it forth and subsequently refined it can fail to look upon any form of totalitarian dictatorship as utterly abhorrent. Nor can I see how anyone with so much as an armchair knowledge of history can fail to comprehend the extent of the difference between the system of government prevailing among Soviet Russia and her satellites and the systems prevailing among the free nations, particularly in the United States. By the same token I am concerned with the way in which the authority of the state has expanded at home and I hope that when this question is presented to you as citizens you will once and for all live down your reputation as a silent generation.

Democracy is the most versatile and resourceful of governments. It has proved itself capable of rising to any occasion, assuming any shape from a laissez-faire economy in time of peace and plenty to a highly efficient military machine in wartime. But there is one principle it can never compromise nor long suspend. This is the principle of the separation of powers. The roots of this principle lie deep in the history of democracy. Madison, in *The Federalist,* called it the "essential precaution in favor of liberty" and "the sacred maxim of free government." "The accumulation of all powers, legislative, executive, and judiciary, in the same hands, whether of one, a few, or many, and whether hereditary, self-appointed, or elective, may justly be pronounced the very definition of tyranny." "It is by balancing each of these powers against the other two," wrote John Adams, "that the efforts in human nature towards tyranny can alone be checked and restrained, and any degree of freedom preserved in the Constitution." Jefferson attached equal weight to the principle. Thus spoke a generation that feared above all the tyranny of the legislature, that expected the tyranny of the executive to come in its day, that set itself against tyranny of all kinds and can now claim a hundred and fifty years of our hindsight to the credit of its foresight. Is this not good reason for asking ourselves whether, in extending the powers and functions of government in the United States, we have faithfully observed—and are now observing—this principle?

But there is a still larger sense in which the growth of the state in a democracy should be a matter of concern to its citizens. There is a yet greater separation of powers that must be observed. What, after all, is the object of political society? Its end and purpose, says Aristotle, "is the good life, and the institutions of social life are means to that end." He defines that good life as "a life of true felicity and goodness"; and he goes on to say, "It is therefore for the sake of good actions, and not for the sake of social life, that political associations must be considered to exist."

This was certainly true of the political association formed in Philadelphia in the summer of 1787. Its founders recognized clearly that government was but one, nor at that the noblest, of several means to their end. ("But what is government itself," says *The Federalist,* "but the greatest of all reflections on human nature? If men were angels no government would be necessary.") They understood both the necessity and the limitations of law. On the near, the safe, side of the fences they erected against tyranny they expected more than mere security for the individual, much more than mere freedom. They expected him to develop his innate qualities of morality and intelligence and to convert these into actions. To these ends they looked upon religion and education as means distinct and separate from government yet essential to it in the total process of achieving the good life.

The theory finds clear and felicitous expression in the Massachusetts Constitution of 1780, whose chief architect and draftsman was John Adams. While guaranteeing the right of citizens to worship according to the dictates of their own consciences, the Constitution pointedly recognizes that "the happiness of a people and the good order and preservation of civil government essentially depend upon piety, religion, and morality" and that "these cannot be generally diffused through a community but by the institution of the public worship of God." It provides for education as follows:

> Wisdom and knowledge, as well as virtue, diffused generally among the body of the people, being necessary for the preservation of their rights and liberties . . . it shall be the duty of legislators and magistrates, in all future periods of this commonwealth, to cherish the interests of literature and the sciences, and all seminaries of them; especially the university at Cambridge, public schools and grammar schools in the towns; to encourage private societies and public institutions . . . ; to countenance and inculcate the principles of humanity and general benevolence, public and private charity, industry and frugality, honesty . . . sincerity, good humor, and all social affections and generous sentiments among the people.

Here clearly was another separation of powers in which raw material that could be protected and perhaps kept alive but could not be refined by government was to be refined by means appropriate to the task. Here, sketched out in John Adams' homely phrases, were the realm of the spirit and the realm of the mind, over which government could exercise sovereignty in only two ways, either as tyrant or as bungler. In either of these ways the cost to society would be the good life and, inevitably, free government. And if the good life and free government should be lost at home, of what avail our efforts against their enemies abroad?

This twofold separation of powers that was held so vital to our country by its founders has lost none of its vitality in a hundred and fifty years. It remains the "sacred maxim of free government," the *sine qua non* of the good life. But if the principle itself is clear, its application is subtle. It is easily overlooked, or cried down, in our hurry to get things done, especially in our anxious preoccupation with the tyranny that bestrides our world and threatens our freedom. It has to be carefully disentangled from business at hand, however urgent, and held as a measure against laws and policies, however meet.

This does not make it easy to invoke our principle. Amid the passions of the hour he who does so may be fiercely challenged. If he is, what authority can he cite, what intellectual and moral company shall he say he keeps? He can cite the Records of the Federal Convention of 1787, the Constitution of the United States, the Federalist Papers, and the correspondence of John Adams and Thomas Jefferson. He can cite the *Politics* of Aristotle and *Two Treatises of Government* by John Locke. He can cite the Gospels according to Matthew, Mark, and Luke. And he can say that he has been keeping company with the authors of these works.

Gentlemen of the graduating class: There are certain things that we can accomplish by law and there are certain things that we cannot accomplish by law or by any process of government. We cannot legislate intelligence. We cannot legislate morality. No, and we cannot legislate loyalty, for loyalty is a kind of morality. We cannot produce these things by decrees or commissions or public inquisitions. The proverbs teach us that

> When wisdom entereth into thine heart, and knowledge is pleasant unto thy soul;
> Discretion shall preserve thee, understanding shall keep thee:
> To deliver thee from the way of the evil man . . .

Wisdom of this kind is born in man. It is awakened in

him by the fear of God. It is cultivated in him and through him put to the uses of society by true religion and liberal education. What was John Adams' charge to the government of Massachusetts? It was not that the government should take it upon itself to organize and manage this process but that the government should respect and give all possible support and encouragement to the schools and colleges and churches whose proper function that was.

There are certain things in man that have to be won, not forced; inspired, not compelled. Among these are many, I should say most, of the things that constitute the good life. You may have to wait awhile, in the army or navy, in professional school or in some great industry or government office before you can fit these things together in poems or policies. But are they not worth living for—and living with—in the meantime? All are essential to democracy. All are proof against its enemies. Wherefore, as we take just and full measure of all authority, let neither time nor the times press us so hard to render unto Caesar the things which are Caesar's that we neglect to render unto God the things that are God's.

Report to the Alumni, 1952-53

(Third annual report, November, 1953)

For the past three years external affairs, particularly those relating to the financing and the rights and responsibilities of universities, have assumed such importance to Yale that I have been at pains to bring them to the attention of the alumni in place of matters more germane to the actual process of education. In my first two annual reports I tried to show Yale's relative position in American (and British) higher education with respect to available and potential economic resources. Last winter I had the honor of serving as chairman of a committee of the Association of American Universities that drew up the report entitled "The Rights and Responsibilities of Universities and Their Faculties." This report, adopted unanimously by the Association and approved by the Yale Corporation, was extensively circulated by the press and reached the alumni in its entirety in the *Alumni Magazine*. In both cases I hoped my efforts would help the alumni arrive at a consensus not only as to basic facts and principles but also as to their ultimate disposition.

Notwithstanding the transcendent importance of these matters, it would be fatal if we allowed them to distract us from recent developments within the process of education itself. For here, as I pointed out at the alumni luncheon last June, we find trends in progress that threaten not only the institutional security of American education but its very mind and spirit. It is high time we took note of these trends. If they are allowed to continue they might easily produce an educational collapse and cultural setback from which neither Yale nor any other university could escape. I propose therefore to devote this report to a discussion of these trends, to show how they affect Yale, to describe what Yale is doing about them and to suggest what else she might be doing.

At the moment the trends show up most vividly in our school system, in acute shortages of schoolrooms and teachers. I have several times referred to these shortages and suggested what they might mean to Yale. But the estimates are constantly being revised upward. The latest I have at hand may be summarized as follows: In 1952–53 our total elementary school enrollment was 25,000,000 and our secondary school enrollment 6,600,000 (including, in both cases, both public and private schools). If the present rate of increase continues as expected it will give us an elementary school enrollment of between 30 and 32 million by 1960, which would project itself into a secondary school enrollment of 11 to 12 million by 1965. We can imagine how this in turn will swell our present higher education enrollment of around 2,000,000.

These trends have already created a shortage of classrooms which, despite our best efforts to date, stands at 325,000 and is expected to increase by another 425,000 by 1960. The results of this shortage are overcrowding, double and often triple sessions, fire and health hazards, and consequent deterioration in discipline and instruction. Far worse is the shortage of teachers. Here we discover the alarming fact that in face of the rapidly increasing enrollment of students the supply of teachers is actually declining. The projected need for properly trained and qualified elementary school teachers in the fall of 1953 was 160,000, against which our colleges produced last year only 36,000. To provide for a secondary school enrollment that is on its way to doubling itself we turned out 86,000 secondary school teachers in 1950; 73,000 in 1951; 61,000 in 1952; and 55,000 in 1953. "The public has been repeatedly advised," declares the 1953 Teacher Supply and Demand Report of the National Education Association, "that the American school system is rapidly moving into a new era. The facts have been literally shouted from the housetops. . . . Yet scarcely anywhere is there evidence of adequate steps being taken to meet this crisis." This arithmetic affords us only a quick barometric reading of conditions which would take another Dickens to depict and will take the best wisdom and energy this country is able to put forth to correct. Their immediate result is a nationwide depreciation of educational standards accompanied by an inordinate waste of human resources.

How does all this affect Yale? Our colleges and universities depend upon the schools for their most essential raw material, and if the schools cannot or do not send them properly qualified material the whole fabric of higher education becomes a bridge built upon rotten pilings. Students who have been hustled through overcrowded and undisciplined classrooms, taught by overworked, underpaid, and improperly qualified teachers, and nurtured on subjects that do not constantly stretch their minds and expand their vision are poor material for college or university. The results of such education cannot fail to undermine the standards of both the liberal arts colleges and the graduate and professional schools of the universities. Nor have they failed to do so.

It is true that the worst effects of the trends cited above should not be felt in higher education for another decade, and it is possible that they may never be felt at Yale. Indeed the reports of our undergraduate deans show constantly improving academic achievement, particularly on the part of public high school graduates. I would make two comments about this achievement. First, it is the exception rather than the rule throughout the country. Second, it is measured by standards which may themselves have become a little corrupted. The two comments may seem to contradict each other. The first implies that Yale's academic standards are higher than the average and that we select, especially from the public schools, better than average students to meet them. To the best of my knowledge and belief, both of these facts are true. That our standards have not been wholly impervious to the crisis in the schools is, I believe, also true.

It was my own recent experience as a teacher in Yale College to find in my classroom each year a growing number of students who, though they might (and did) score high marks for their knowledge of the subject of the course, might have failed it altogether if I had graded them in rhetoric. Before me as I write is the annual report of the dean of one of our professional schools which complains of "widespread illiteracy among college graduates . . . want of competence effectively to read, write and spell the English language and even more to read, spell or write any foreign language . . . accordingly . . . want of capacity to acquire and apply intelligence." Beside it is a letter from a professor of economics, a distinguished graduate of European universities and former member of their faculties who has taught at both Yale and Harvard, expressing dismay at the "near illiteracy" of his graduate students in both institutions. "Few of them," he says, "know how to write, and some don't even know how to read. The main trouble undoubtedly lies with our primary and secondary education, and I am not sure how much of it could still be remedied by appropriate reforms in our undergraduate curriculum. I am afraid it may be too late by then to make up some of the deficiencies in the students' earlier training. Still, it has to be attempted . . ." With half our undergraduates now entering professional schools and nearly all undergoing some form of professional or quasi-professional training after graduation, the urgency of the attempt is indicated.

I have selected this evidence from our own faculty at random. I could multiply it many times from business and industrial as well as professional and academic sources. I might go on to show that the conditions it reveals at Yale are not as bad as they are elsewhere. That would be a poor way to make them appear satisfactory at Yale. It proves, I think, that in education as in commerce, when bad money gets into circulation it drives out good, and the process is only intensified as the latter is hoarded. Yale can neither profit by other people's misfortunes nor isolate herself from their effects. That these should be felt as keenly at Yale as they are today suggests what might happen if they should continue unabated until 1960.

I have cited the two most obvious causes of these conditions: the shortage of facilities and the shortage of teachers. The criticism I have quoted from Yale sources points to a third cause, less obvious, perhaps, but certainly no less important. This is the decline of the liberal arts as a force in our national educational system. These studies are disappearing under a layer of vocational and other substitutes like the landscape in the ice age, only this glacier reaches from coast to coast and border to border. With all due exceptions, of which Yale is and I believe will continue to be one, and all honor and power to those exceptions, the attitude of most educational institutions toward this trend varies from mild concern to indifference and cheerful acquiescence.

Alas, no substitutes have been found for reading and writing. The practice and enjoyment of these skills in an ever widening orbit and on an ever ascending plane are both ends and means to the liberal arts. If deficiencies in the skills show up in colleges and even in the highly selective graduate schools of universities, do they not betray a comprehensive deficiency of the parent discipline? At a meeting of the Association of American Universities last year a distinguished dean from another institution, deploring the phenomenon, attributed it to the failure of the schools. I have heard school teachers blame it on the colleges. The argument moves in a vicious circle, leaving untouched the central fact that both schools and colleges and through them American civilization are denying themselves the benefits of studies which, for two thousand years, throughout western civilization, have been esteemed as the key to the good life as well as to all true academic achievement.

The point is substantiated by more disturbing evidence. While over half the nation's youth finishes high school and a fifth (of the whole) goes on to some form of higher education, this group includes less than half of those best qualified for such education. Of the top quarter in intellectual ability, 20 per cent do not continue for financial reasons, and 40 per cent—a proportion exactly equal to that which does continue—for lack of motivation.

That so large a proportion of our best college material eschews higher education for such a reason is a fact that requires much interpretation. It is a composite of environment, chance, social status, geography, and other elements and influences. Is it not, too, further proof of our neglect of the liberal arts? The whole impulse and tendency of the liberal arts is to encourage the individual to make the most of all educational opportunities within reach and constantly to seek new ones. If the parents and teachers of these "unmotivated" young men and women had themselves been steeped in the liberal arts would they not have communicated this impulse to their children and students? If their schools had afforded anything like proper introductions to the liberal arts, would the impulse have been lost? The voluntary rejection of higher education by so many Americans capable of profiting by it proves to my satisfaction at least that the grain cannot grow where the seed has not been planted. We can only speculate as to how much talent is wasted in the process—certainly much that would bring credit to Yale and benefit to society. This is another measure of the practical price society pays for its impractical evaluation of the liberal arts.

We are confused over the very meaning of the phrase, let alone the subjects of study for which it stands. It has acquired connotations of special privilege and preciosity. At the risk of laboring the obvious, therefore, let us recall that, as it is used here, the word "liberal" comes from the Latin *liber,* meaning "free"; that the proper meaning of the phrase "liberal arts" is "the arts becoming to a free man"; and that from earliest times these have included the sciences (in the Middle Ages, arithmetic, geometry, and astronomy).* In other words the liberal arts are rooted in freedom, not privilege, and they are broad, not narrow, in educational scope.

It is true that both Greek and medieval society restricted to a minority the number of those who were truly free, hence fully qualified as beneficiaries of the arts becoming a free man. In Greek times, these were the guardians of a fundamentally undemocratic society; in medieval times, aristocrats, clergy, and wandering scholars. It is also true that this identification of the liberal arts with special orders of society dies hard in modern Britain and Europe. It grew out of a constricting interpretation of the meaning of freedom rather than a constriction inherent in the meaning of the liberal arts, and it gained currency in the United States through inverted snobbism as well as ignorance of the facts. It is as much at variance with our cardinal principle of equal opportunity as it is with the true meaning of the liberal arts.

The notion that the liberal arts are for the *rara avis* is

* The others were grammar, rhetoric, logic and music.

no less difficult to explain though often more difficult to dispel. Perhaps it is attributable to the rather narrow, literal meaning our workaday society attaches to the word "arts." Thus the busy father discussing college with his son advises against "impractical" courses that will not help him in business. Or the scientist or engineer stresses professional purposes with which he believes the liberal arts to be incompatible. In this the champions of the liberal arts themselves have not been altogether blameless. They have been guilty of smugness and at times have seemed content to live on rote and reputation. Such, for example, appears to have been the case in British education in 1835 when Macaulay wrote in desperation:

> Give a boy Robinson Crusoe. That is worth all the grammars of rhetoric and logic in the world. . . . Who ever reasoned better for having been taught the difference between a syllogism and an enthymeme? Who ever composed with greater spirit and elegance because he could define an oxymoron or an aposiopesis? I am not joking but writing quite seriously when I say that I would much rather order a hundred copies of Jack the Giant-Killer for our schools than a hundred copies of any grammar of rhetoric or logic that ever was written.

The same impatience with a curriculum whose claims were pretentious but whose elements and purposes had become obscure heralded the advent of the elective system in our own schools and colleges half a century later.

All these impressions of the liberal arts rest upon a quantitative fallacy. They emphasize content as distinct from quality and spirit. If the critic reasons on this basis he may discount the liberal arts as severely as Dickens'

Mr. Podsnap, who thought they should represent, reflect, and conduce to "getting up at eight, shaving close at a quarter-past, breakfasting at nine, going to the City at ten, coming home at half-past five, and dining at seven. Nothing else to be permitted to those same vagrants the Arts, on pain of excommunication." Or, evidently, as their exemplars were doing when Macaulay found them exuberating in oxymorons and enthymemes and plumped for *Robinson Crusoe*. Or as the scientist does who forgets that science is part of the liberal arts; or the professional man who asks what Greek or Latin have to do with law or medicine or engineering.

The purpose of the liberal arts is not to teach businessmen business, or grammarians grammar, or college students Greek and Latin (which have disappeared from their required curricula). It is to awaken and develop the intellectual and spiritual powers in the individual before he enters upon his chosen career, so that he may bring to that career the greatest possible assets of intelligence, resourcefulness, judgment, and character. It is, in John Stuart Mill's telling phrase, to make "capable and cultivated human beings." "Men are men," Mill said, "before they are lawyers or physicians or manufacturers; and if you make them capable and sensible men they will make themselves capable and sensible lawyers or physicians." I know of no better statement of the purpose of the liberal arts nor any that so firmly establishes their place in a national educational system that is dedicated, as ours is, to the preparation of men and women not just for intellectual pursuits but for life.

From this statement we may proceed as Mill himself did to the conclusion that the liberal arts and many of the studies thought to be in competition with them are not competitors but allies. This was Mill's pronouncement on the conflict that raged in his day between the "old classical studies" and the "new scientific studies." Mill denied that this conflict had any foundation in principle whatsoever, declaring that "it is only the stupid inefficiency of the usual teaching which makes those studies be regarded as competitors instead of allies." There is even less reason for such a conflict of principles today. The "old classical studies" have been greatly enriched by the infusion of history, philosophy, literature, language, and the fine arts into the erstwhile domain of the grammarian and logician. Scientific studies never were "new" to the liberal arts, as they claimed three of the original seven. The social studies—economics, anthropology, political science, sociology, psychology—have found their place in the sun alongside of language and literature. The very term "liberal arts" has given way in professional academic usage to the term "general education," with its obviously broader implications as to content and method. Every trade, profession, and vocation has an equal interest in "capable and cultivated human beings." How could this represent a conflict of principle?

It does not. The idea of a conflict of principle represents ignorance of the facts with its usual by-products of misunderstanding and prejudice. That this is so should give us courage to attack these ancient enemies of learning. But where do we begin? With the conditions cited at the beginning of this report—the shortage of schoolrooms, the dearth of teachers? What can Yale do about them? Could we not turn our backs on them and count on our reputation to bring us our quota of exceptional or specially privileged individual students? Quite apart from its morality when viewed in the light of our charter, our aims and ideals as a national university, and our tax-exempt status, such a policy would surely defeat itself. We have seen how the general deterioration of educational standards is already being felt in our undergraduate and professional schools. To turn our backs on this would be to court disaster. For our own sake as well as for the country's we must face it and do something about it.

We must and we can. Though we cannot produce a magic formula that will relieve the shortages of schoolrooms and teachers, we can do a number of things that will contribute to those results. Above all I would name two: First, we can maintain the liberal arts in the fullest possible health and vigor at Yale, and second, we can capitalize them as a motivating force in American education by improving and expanding our liberal arts training program for secondary school teachers. Both steps would lead directly to improved conditions in the schools as well as at Yale. For of this I am convinced: that if this country is to be shaken out of the trance that blinds it to the needs of its educational system, the great awakening will be brought about by parents and teachers steeped in the liberal arts and imbued with their spirit. It is both the duty and the opportunity of Yale to make this experience rich and fruitful for her own students and, through them, to bring this spirit powerfully to the assistance of American education.

I have spoken thus far of things we might and should be doing, as though we were not doing them at the moment. This is not true. In the last stages of the second World War a number of universities, Yale among them, sensing that all was not well in higher education, undertook to re-examine its fundamental principles and purposes. All were concerned with the same basic problem I have endeavored to state in these pages, namely the provision of a general, nonspecialized liberal arts program for their undergraduate students as a foundation for later undergraduate and graduate specialization. Out of such studies at Yale, Harvard, Columbia, Chicago and elsewhere came significant reports, prescribing (and setting in motion) much curricular revision and reorganization. It is regrettable, I think, that the Yale report, unlike the others mentioned, was never published, for it partook of the same quality and offered comment of no less general significance. At all events it ushered in a period of soul-searching and self-criticism on the part of our own faculty which has already produced notable results and which still continues.

Constructive as it has been, however, this stirring and searching has not closed the gap in our educational system. Its results have created something of a charmed circle within the orbit of higher education, and even here they have been neither exclusive nor conclusive. Side by side with the new programs, inconsistent practices have continued to flourish, and the programs themselves have been subject to frequent revision. By attacking the problem on an institutional rather than an individual basis, they failed to come to grips with the phase of it that lay within the orbit of secondary education. Whatever they may have accomplished elsewhere in particular or elsewhere in general (and I think what I say here is true for the country at large), at Yale they left this unfinished business: they continued to let too many students slip by, via detours and double standards; they failed to provide adequately, at either end, for the transition between school and college; and they contained no plans for the transfusion of the liberal arts into secondary education by schoolteachers properly oriented and trained for that purpose. But the interest of higher education in the liberal arts had been revived and a general education program that would redeem that interest had been started, and this was a great step forward.

The next step was forced upon us by the Korean war. The prospect of "peacetime" military service, whether through Selective Service or some form of universal military training and service, showed us, no longer abstractly but concretely, the indivisible responsibility of school and college in matters of general education. Students confronted by two years in the armed forces plus four of college and three or more of professional school began to look around desperately for vocational or "preprofessional" offerings—anything that would speed up the interminable apprenticeship that stood between them and their projected careers. This, by the way, has been a universal trend, even in such traditional homes of the liberal arts as Great Britain and France. It has meant a universal setback for the liberal arts. That these countries should also be suffering from the trend is another and a compelling reason why we should take it seriously. At home it seemed as though the liberal arts were being ground between an upper millstone of vocationalism to which the weight of military service had now been added and a nether millstone of public indifference. The educational mill was grinding out skilled but uneducated human beings, American citizens who by Mill's standards were capable but uncultivated, Yale graduates who were deficient in reading and writing.

There was a gap somewhere and it had to be closed.

Where was it? The colleges said, in the schools. The schools said, in the colleges. Both were right. Throughout the vast majority of our secondary schools, as I have already pointed out, the liberal arts were being smothered by vocationalism. But for this the colleges were themselves partly responsible. The elective rebellion against the old liberal arts college curriculum had run wild, and colleges were giving academic credit for everything from philosophy to fly fishing. With the colleges setting such standards, how could the schools in their almost infinite diversity and their susceptibility to the moods of local boards be expected to do better? There are 75,000 public-school districts in the United States, each one a highly and often pridefully autonomous community. The public high schools in these communities are attended by 92 per cent of the nation's youth enrolled in secondary education. Of the remainder, some 6 or 7 per cent attend private denominational institutions, and only 2 per cent or less private nondenominational. With this basic diversity, with only 40 per cent of the top quarter of the graduates of all these institutions sufficiently motivated to move on into any form of higher education, how could the colleges reproach the schools for neglecting Shakespeare for bookkeeping and automobile driving? What about the colleges who maintained million dollar gate receipts by giving football players academic credit for scrimmaging and basketball players credit for rhythms and tap dancing? So the argument raged across the country, a jumble of values and standards through which the properly motivated schoolboy picked his way with all the intrepidity of the early explorers, and Yale groped for her true and proper bearings.

In one way our problem was less difficult than that of

many other colleges and universities, in another way more so. It was less difficult in that we still drew over half of our undergraduates from schools that were as eager as we were to redefine and revive the liberal arts in a viable program of general education. It was more difficult in that we were, by virtue of this fact, less influenced by the state of affairs in public secondary education, hence less aware of it and less well equipped to do anything about it. In fact, as I have already mentioned, we were somewhat blinded to that state of affairs by the remarkable performance of the public high school graduates who now comprised over 40 per cent of our own student body, a highly deceptive manifestation representing a highly selected and exceptional group of students.

It was natural, therefore, that we should take the first deliberate step toward solution of the problem in the company of old friends. This we did by participating with Harvard and Princeton, and Andover, Exeter, and Lawrenceville, three secondary schools that for years had sent the majority of their graduates to the three colleges and had closely cooperated with them in matters of curriculum, in a fresh study of the content and location of general education in the national educational system. The study was launched in 1950 by the headmaster, faculty, and members of the Alumni Educational Policy Committee of Andover and carried on during 1951–52 by a committee representing the six institutions on a grant from the Fund for the Advancement of Education. The whole project was known as the School and College Study of General Education.

The results of the study were published last fall under the title *General Education in School and College*, a book which has already attracted much attention in educational circles and, I am glad to say, among our alumni. It has many excellent features including clarity and brevity, and offers a number of significant conclusions of which I would here stress the following: First and foremost, it recognizes general education as essential to higher education, and the liberal arts as the essential ingredients of general education. Second, it recognizes once and for all that in the American system general education is the joint responsibility of secondary school and college, a unit consisting of the last two years of school and the first two years of college. From this it deduces (third) the imperative need for a smooth, orderly, and constantly ascending progression (the committee calls it "progression in strength") for the student in general education. Fourth, it finds this process at present cluttered and obstructed with waste, slow motion, duplication, and cross purposes, all frustrating and demoralizing to the student and inclining him to seek relief from boredom in extracurricular activities or vocational short cuts to his career. Fifth, of special interest in the light of conclusions drawn from motivation statistics earlier in this report, it holds that "the greatest single failure which appears from the evidence of our study is a failure to communicate to students the full meaning and purpose of a liberal education." And finally, for us to read in the same light, it declares, "The obvious should be stated at once. A love for learning depends overwhelmingly upon the personality, skill, knowledge and communicable enthusiasm of the individual teacher." These conclusions are buttressed by questionnaires submitted to recent graduates of the three schools and translated into educational policy in a number of specific programs for the components of general education: English, foreign languages, mathematics, the natural sciences, history, literature, etc. In short, the book defines the problem of general education more concretely than it had been defined to date, and makes eminently practical suggestions for its solution.

In various ways in addition to those mentioned we did what we could at Yale to cooperate with and encourage this undertaking. In June 1952, when the committee's final report was about ready for publication, I appointed a committee representing both the Freshman and College faculties and the Corporation, to take up the question where the university studies and reports of a decade ago and the new School and College Committee report left off, to study their implications for Yale, and to make recommendations to the faculty. A year later, the Committee completed the first phase of its work with a Report on General Education.

We hope the report may guide Yale in completing the essential first step toward a solution of the national problem of general education as I have outlined it in these pages, namely, to ensure that our part of the bargain, the two college years of general education, will be as rewarding as possible for all who enter it. We hope it will lead to a true progression in strength for our freshmen and sophomores consistent with our own standards and traditions and at the same time significant as an example in American education generally.

To provide a counterpart for secondary school teachers, without which the undergraduate program of general education would be but one crutch where two are needed, we have not gone as far as we have with our undergraduate plans, though here too we have not been idle. As one of two universities (the other is Columbia) participating in the John Hay Whitney Foundation program of graduate fellowships in the humanities, and through our own Master of Arts in Teaching program, we have cast shadows of what I hope will be even greater coming events.

Of all branches of the liberal arts none is in such poor health in the United States as the humanities. These are the studies which for centuries have sustained the spirit of learning and the ends, as well as the means, of civilization. Yet of all studies, in the evaluation of a practical people, these are considered the least practical. For this reason motivation of the student becomes all-important. It must come at the right time, and from teachers not only eager but properly prepared to give it. Otherwise, save in exceptional cases, it will not come at all. Once again, all signs point to secondary school teachers, particularly those in public high schools where the tradition of the humanities is weakest, the attitude of parents and students least congenial to their development, and the practical opportunities of teachers anxious to further such development most restricted. To provide for their needs the Whitney Foundation established a program of graduate fellowships in the humanities which brings to the graduate school of each of the participating universities ten public high school teachers selected by merit on a regional basis. At Yale these teachers spend a year of study and close personal association with our own outstanding teachers and scholars in their fields. They are thus brought up to date on professional developments in those fields and given fresh perspectives on problems they must face when they return to their schools.

The Whitney Foundation program is now in its second year. While it is too soon yet to judge its ultimate results, at Yale it has had an auspicious beginning. The comments of the Fellows have been enthusiastic and of their instructors even more so. It is very evident that both believe they have been actively furthering a vital process that will yield results where results are most sorely needed.

Our Master of Arts in Teaching represents a more comprehensive effort to bridge the gap between general education in school and college through the training of teachers. This program has grown out of plans which I drew up and submitted to the Carnegie Corporation in the fall of 1950. The plans called for a small, essentially experimental program whose purpose was to inject as much as possible of the actual substance of the liberal arts into the training of secondary school teachers while at the same time giving them the essentials of pedagogy that would enable them to meet their professional requirements. As compared with teacher training programs prevailing throughout the country, ours would redress the balance between the liberal arts and pedagogical methodology in favor of the liberal arts. The whole was conceived primarily in the interests of public high school teachers, and a systematic effort was to be made to recruit candidates from our own and other liberal arts colleges.

As might be expected of any project that took such difficult objectives for its goal and advanced to meet them on such a modest and frankly experimental basis, it has sometimes seemed like bailing out the ocean. Yet it has yielded solid results. Whatever value these may hold for the nation, their value to Yale is inestimable. They have shown us more clearly than we have ever seen them before not merely the outlines but the concrete detail of the curriculum we must support, if Yale is to play the role in secondary and higher education projected in these pages. They have shown us the things we must do if Yale is to play the part in restoring the liberal arts as an educational force required in her own interests and desperately needed by American society.

To accomplish this purpose the Master of Arts in Teaching must not only be maintained in its present form. It must be strengthened and expanded. Bridges must be built between it and our public school system. More vigorous recruitment of candidates for the program than has been possible to date must be undertaken. The whole program must receive the general support of the entire faculty, with the same clear sense of direction that has guided its present faculty and administrative staff—a platoon where an army is needed.

These are not new aims in the history and tradition of Yale. They are the fulfillment of old aims, aims neglected or not clearly seen in the confused perspective of present-day education. Yale has always sent her graduates into the teaching profession. In preparing candidates for university teaching our Graduate School has been preeminent. It awarded the first Ph.D. degree in the United States (1861) and since then has maintained a qualitative record in this particular phase of teacher training second to none. Since its founding in 1907 our Department of Education has turned out a small annual quota of men and women trained in public-school administration. Each year a handful of our own seniors takes up school teaching, the great majority in private preparatory schools. These are all honorable precedents for the more systematic and much more vigorous liberal arts program for secondary school teachers the times call for today. We must honor those precedents. We can and we must rise to the occasion.

Rising to the occasion requires an unusually clear sense of purpose. To organize and carry out our twofold program of general education for undergraduates and secondary school teachers, particularly the teacher training part of it, will require new endowment, new working capital that will not tie our hands by multifarious conditions and restrictions or expire at the end of a term. This is not a tentative promotional project. It is a specific long-term purpose that must be incorporated in the University's regular life and work and supported by our own resources. It is essential to see it as such in order to provide the resources that will make it possible in the first place.

We must see just as clearly the position it must occupy in our educational scheme of things if it is to be effective. It must occupy the same place in our scale of values as the best we offer in undergraduate and graduate education. To secure this place consensus is needed as much as it is in the provision of resources. Yale is a diversified and highly individualistic community, in which conflict of interests, particularly in competition for resources, is perpetual and sharp, and a minority of one may consider a majority of ninety-nine a tyranny. It would be illusory to expect each one of those interests to attach equal importance to this program. Yet in this as in all things Yale is a community, and communities order their life and work by consensus. We must all see this purpose clearly even though we may not all see it whole.

We must see it, also, as part of the deficit of Yale, a part that is not and by nature cannot be included in fiscal reports. I mean Yale's educational deficit, the balance between her educational obligations and what she is doing to fulfill them. For all the financial resources we have recruited during the past three years, our long-run educational deficit remains disproportionately large. Another item in this deficit is facilities for teaching and research that will keep our sciences in *their* proper place in our educational scheme of things. I have before me as I write requests and demands for similar facilities from no less than thirty-one schools and departments in the University, each one translated into educational terms and put to me in language as urgent as the scientists'. We have not yet finished correcting our faculty salary scale, particularly in the lower ranks, an item that is directly and categorically educational and whose weight is felt and expressed by every department.

Outside of this categorically educational deficit but inside the same limited supply of resources, we face an accumulated and steadily growing deficit in the maintenance of our plant—long-deferred repairs and replacements that must soon be effected or cost us the loss of irreplaceable capital assets. Merely to keep things going as they are we must meet a combined payroll of salaries and wages of nearly a million dollars a month. Moreover this payroll is subject to all the pressures such as competition with other institutions and forms of employment, collective bargaining and strikes, felt by a profit-making corporation. Each of these needs must be seen in its proper perspective by a community whose foremost concern must be continued leadership and progression in the educational field.

Such are the institutional circumstances in which I say we can and must restore the liberal arts as a force in American education. I say we can because again and again in Yale's long history a sense of common purpose—at times articulate, at times subconscious—has enabled us to resolve conflicting interests in constructive policy: otherwise our history might not have been so long. I say we must because the present purpose lays an equal obligation on every member of Yale as it does upon every American: the obligation of ensuring for his children full value in the promise of equal opportunity in education.